Stop feeling invisible and start attracting the attention you deserve.

WRITER
GET
NOTICED!

A STRENGTHS-BASED APPROACH TO CREATING
A STANDOUT AUTHOR PLATFORM

COLLEEN M. STORY

MIDCHANNEL PRESS
www.midchannelpress.com

Although every precaution has been taken to verify the accuracy of the information contained herein, including Internet addresses, the author and publisher assume no responsibility for any errors or omissions. Further, the publisher does not have any control over and does not assume any responsibility for author or third-party websites or their content.

No liability is assumed for damages that may result from the use of information contained within. The author does not dispense medical advice or prescribe the use of any technique as a form of treatment for physical, emotional, or medical problems without the advice of a physician, either directly or indirectly. The intent of the author is only to offer information of a general nature to help you in your quest for physical, emotional, and creative well-being. In the event you use any of the information in this book for yourself, the author and the publisher assume no responsibility for your actions.

Books may be ordered through booksellers or by contacting the publisher at:

Midchannel Press
P.O. Box 52133
Idaho Falls, ID 83402
www.midchannelpress.com

Email: publisher@midchannelpress.com

To receive a free weekly email newsletter delivering tips and updates about putting the power of *you* behind your best creative life, register directly at www.writingandwellness.com/newsletter. For more information on creatively building a successful author business, please see www.writerceo.com.

Cover Design: Damonza.com

Interior Design: Damonza.com

ISBN 13: 978-0-9990991-2-4 (Paperback edition)

ISBN 13: 978-0-9990991-3-1 (eBook edition)

Library-of-Congress Control Number: 2018914012

First Edition: March 2019, printed in the U.S.A.

Also by Colleen M. Story

Loreena's Gift

Overwhelmed Writer Rescue

For more information, please see:

colleenmstory.com

writingandwellness.com

writerceo.com

Stop feeling invisible and start attracting the attention you deserve.

WRITER GET NOTICED!

A STRENGTHS-BASED APPROACH TO CREATING A STANDOUT AUTHOR PLATFORM

CONTENTS

Part III | 191

INTRODUCTION

Most writers, when they first start out, think of only one thing: writing a bestselling book.

It's what I thought about. When the writing bug first bit me, I dreamed of seeing my book in bookstores. I imagined what the cover might look like and how the weight of the paper would feel in my hands. I longed for validation from a publisher and positive feedback from readers. These thoughts sustained me through years of trial and error as I learned how to write a publishable story.

I didn't realize back then that my dreams were far too limited. I was a victim of small thinking.

Like most beginning writers, I was locked into a youthful mindset similar to the way students are at the end of their high school years. Looking out on their future, they may think, *I'm going to be a doctor ... an architect ... a teacher ... an astronaut.* But most aren't really sure what they're going to end up doing, especially at that young age. They can't be. They don't understand the world and the wide array of possibilities that exist within it. They don't understand themselves, and all the many gifts they have to explore.

New writers are the same. We strike out with some vague idea of what our future is going to look like: *I'm going to be a writer. I'm going to publish a bestseller.*

It sounds good, and for a while it may work if it keeps you writing. Heck, it may even be enough to get you that publishing contract you want, that self-publishing business you've dreamed of, or even that bestseller, and you'll go on happy as a clam.

For many of you, however—I suspect, most of you reading this book—you're going to experience a number of setbacks and disappointments along the way, and that dream is going to wear thin. Eventually, you may wind up in a place where you feel discouraged, fatigued, and confused. Was this the future you had in mind?

Maybe you've been writing for years and you still haven't gotten that publishing contract you wanted. Maybe you *did* publish, but your book didn't sell well, and you struggled to keep going. Maybe you self-published, but found the earnings weren't what you'd hoped, and you started to wonder if this writing thing was for you after all. Maybe you blogged for years and your readership barely increased. Maybe you tried marketing tactic after marketing tactic with few results.

Whatever your story—and we all have one—if you've come to this point feeling less than fulfilled, this book is for you.

This is the book you should have had way back when you first thought about being a writer—when you thought you understood what that meant. Write a book. Publish it. Find readers. Make money. Be happy.

But that's small thinking. That's high school thinking. It's time to move beyond that to a place where you *can* find true fulfillment in your writing career. That place is out there. You just haven't found it yet, and even more importantly, in your search for it, you've probably been going the wrong direction.

How do I know? I've traveled that journey. I've wasted precious years with small thinking that kept my creative wings tied behind my back. I worked hard, and I was stubborn enough to keep going. I experienced some success as a result, and maybe you have, too, but I also experienced plenty of despair, setbacks, discouragements, and self-doubt that kept me from finding the fulfilling career I enjoy today.

Most of us go about it all wrong. We think the first thing we must do is write a publishable book. But that sort of thinking can lead to years of struggle, failure, and waning enthusiasm, plus an overall nagging feeling that you just don't know what you're doing. That was the old way, and it doesn't work anymore. That was the outdated way, the "take-three-times-as-long-as-you-need-to-get-where-you-want-to-be" way.

It's time for a new paradigm.

It's time to take a brand-new approach to your writing career, the type of approach that employs not only "big" thinking, but a strengths-based attitude about who you are and what you can bring to the world. It's time to create an author platform uniquely right for *you*, that uses your gifts and talents and the skills you can easily develop to produce not only something you can be proud of, but something that touches others and expands your reach in a rewarding and fulfilling way.

In today's publishing world, platform is the key not only to the success of your books, but to your personal and professional fulfillment as a creative entrepreneur. When you discover a platform that reflects who you really are, you'll also find a writing career that gets you up in the morning, eager for the day—a career you truly love.

A NOTE TO THE READER

Before you dive into chapter one, I have one important suggestion for you: *do all the exercises*. Rather than just the author of this book, I want to be your coach, and help guide you through the process of finding your unique niche as a writer. Beyond that, I want to help you create a platform that fits you perfectly. Though you could simply read the book and learn some important lessons, I guarantee you'll gain a lot more if you work with me as we go.

If you're serious about creating a platform that helps you stand out in the crowd, you'll need to invest some time and effort, but trust me, it will be fun! As your coach, I'll help you find increased writing success, and you'll be much happier with the results. So grab a new notebook you can write in or open up a new folder on your laptop so you're prepared to brainstorm, answer some questions, and jot down some important notes as we go.

This book is for all independent writers, no matter what type of writing you do. If you write books, magazine articles, short stories, essays, and/or poems, or if you're a freelance writer/editor with your own business working for various clients, you'll find what you need to improve your odds of "getting noticed" in these pages. If you work for an employer and you're happy there, some of the following chapters may not apply to you, but if you eventually want to work for yourself, you've definitely come to the right place.

The process is pretty straightforward. Just go from one chapter to the next, and I'll guide you on a journey of self-discovery that will help you find the unique creative gold that is your ideal author platform, from which you can grow a thriving, successful business.

Ready? Pull out your notebook. This is going to be fun.

A Crow was jealous of the Raven, because he was considered a bird of good omen and always attracted the attention of men, who noted by his flight the good or evil course of future events. Seeing some travelers approaching, the Crow flew up into a tree, and perching herself on one of the branches, cawed as loudly as she could. The travelers turned towards the sound and wondered what it foreboded, when one of them said to his companion, "Let us proceed on our journey, my friend, for it is only the caw of a crow, and her cry, you know, is no omen."

Those who assume a character that does not belong to them, only make themselves ridiculous.

~Aesop's Fables Online Collection, www.aesopfables.com/aesop1.html

PART I
ARE YOU GOING
THE RIGHT WAY?

*"Not until we are lost do we begin
to understand ourselves."*

~HENRY DAVID THOREAU

CHAPTER 1

PURSUING YOUR OWN PATH

H AVE YOU EVER looked up to another writer, admired her success, and said to yourself, "That's what I need to do. I'll just follow what *she* did."

It's a common way of thinking, and in most cases, a good way. We naturally learn from observing others, and it's always helpful to study those who have reached the level of success we aspire to. The problem comes from expecting if you do exactly what this other person did, you'll accomplish the same level of success. That's a symptom of small thinking, and it rarely works. In fact, this sort of outlook often leads to discouragement and despair rather than success. When you do (or think you did) everything the successful author did, and the same rewards refuse to come your way, you may feel like a failure. But in truth, you didn't fail. You just followed a path that wasn't meant for you.

Consider how many variables there are in life. To start, no two people are the same. You don't have the same talents, gifts, or personality as someone else. You are *you*, and that means you must forge your own path to success.

Yes, you can absolutely pick up tips from others, learn important skills from them, study as an apprentice, and use your newly acquired knowledge to take giant steps forward in your career … as long as you go about it with the right mindset, understanding that all you're doing is picking up tools to make *your* journey a little easier.

But if you think, even for one minute, that following in another's steps will take you to the top of that same mountain of success, you're making a huge mistake. We all have our own mountains to climb. You have to find yours.

There's a Limit to the Benefits of Following Others

You may have already tried following in the steps of others, only to end up discouraged and depressed. Maybe you got your master's degree in fiction writing, because your teachers told you that was a good idea, and after graduation found yourself confused and wondering what to do next. Perhaps you self-published because, hey, that's what writers are doing these days, and you didn't want to wait for a traditional publisher. You worked hard on your book, but upon release, the response wasn't as enthusiastic as you'd hoped. A year later, yes, you had a book on Amazon, but not much else to show for it.

Maybe you published a few books to positive sales, but then things started going downhill, and you don't know why. Marketing classes didn't help and now you feel discouraged by the whole process.

It's moments like these when you need to realize that following what others tell you to do gets you only so far and may even slow you down. The only thing that will take you where you want to go is a thorough knowledge of yourself, what you really want, and what strengths you possess. Unfortunately, few writers have this insight, so they continue to flounder without ever getting where they want to be.

Today's Writing Career Looks Different than It Did Years Ago

An independent writing career today looks much different than it did fifty years ago, or even twenty years ago. Technology has changed things, and whatever you may think about it (good or bad), it has opened up new possibilities as to what you can do within the overarching term of being a "writer."

Career possibilities for today's writers are plentiful and varied. Here are just a few of the options:

- Biographer
- Blogger
- Book reviewer
- Comic book (graphic novel) writer
- Copywriter
- Editor
- Essay writer
- Food/arts/music/movie reviewer
- Freelance writer
- Ghostwriter
- Grant writer

- Greeting card writer

- Journalist

- Literary agent

- Marketing communications specialist

- Novelist

- Playwright

- Poet or lyricist

- Proofreader

- Proposal writer

- Publicist

- Teacher or professor

- Technical writer

- Travel writer

- Speechwriter

- Social media manager

- Translator

- Writing tutor

- Writing coach

- Video game writer

Clearly, a writer has many more options today than to simply write books. The exciting thing is you can write books and also branch out and tackle other writing projects too. Most writers these days wear many hats, and that's not a bad thing. Turns out that developing other skills has a way of making your author platform more noticeable and your writing career even more fulfilling.

Writers Today Wear a Number of Hats

Although books often form the foundation of any writing career, a writer's "reach" doesn't have to end there. Many writers augment their incomes by writing articles, blog posts, grants, proposals, or for online courses. Some write for corporations or small businesses, while others lend their talents to nonprofit organizations. Still others teach writing, speak at writer's workshops, create writing products to sell, or grow and sell successful, content-heavy websites. There are so many options—you only have to use your imagination.

Being good at more than one thing—even if they're related—is a blessing in today's market. If you limit yourself to only writing books, you open yourself up to an enormous amount of competition where only the top one percent stand out. If you have multiple talents and related skills, however—which most writers have—and use them to reach more people, you'll find it's much easier to create a unique niche that sets you apart and helps you build a robust following.

"Oftentimes," wrote editor, writer, and human rights lecturer Natalie Jesionka on career-finding site *The Muse*, "one path can be a building block for something else, and it can help you gain critical experience that'll someday propel you toward another career goal.... We live in a world where we can run a startup, have a day job, and work remotely at night if we want to—so why not take advantage of it?"

Think Bigger

It's easy to become trapped in "small thinking." Our ideas are boxed in by what we've been conditioned to believe is the true writer's life, complete with cabins on lakes and months of quiet time to create our masterpieces.

Today's writer, however, diversifies. She may be a writer *and* an editor, a writer and a publisher, a writer and a graphic artist, a writer and an advocate, a writer and a therapist, a writer and a teacher, and the list goes on. We can look at this from one perspective and say, "Gosh, it's a shame most writers can't make a living writing books anymore." But you're boxing yourself in by thinking writing equals books only. That's a limited point of view, and it's not the kind that will help you get ahead.

Instead, look at the opportunities and say, "Wow, writers are able to do so many things with their talents. They can write and publish books and also branch out into other creative outlets, all of which have the potential to provide additional audiences and income. The sky is truly the limit."

The Way of the Future: More than One Purpose?

You've probably heard you need to find your "purpose." There are quizzes, blogs, and workshops designed to help you find your one true calling. We've been told once we discover this key to our destiny, then the rest of our lives will fall in line easily and meaningfully, and the world will open up to us.

I bought into that idea for a while, but now I doubt the wisdom of finding my one and only purpose. It's no longer about doing only this *or only* that. Today's world is all about this *and that.* Foundation that's also moisturizer. Pants that easily convert into shorts. Tablets that morph into laptops. Writers who are also entrepreneurs: authorpreneurs.

In fact, if you've had trouble finding your one and only purpose, you may actually have the advantage. If today is about this *and that*—and I'm theorizing it is—then limiting yourself to just one purpose ("I'm a writer!") may be limiting your potential and leading you down a road that's not really yours.

Many of us enjoy exploring and using multiple talents. Breaking out of the box is liberating for the creative mind, and is the best option for long-term writing and creative success.

Think of the people in your life who have followed multiple paths, or chosen different purposes at different times. One of my good friends worked first as a missionary, then a writer for a corporation, and now homeschools her kids. Another friend is a photographer for a wood company, a music teacher, a talented flute player, and holds a degree in microbiology. Yet another is an information technology guru for public schools, blows a wicked trumpet, and composes his own orchestra music. All of these people followed their multiple talents and ended up successful and happy.

If writing is your purpose, don't let it limit you. You can use your writing to do so many good things in the world, so I'm suggesting you broaden your mind to take in every interest, skill, and passion you encounter. As you find ways to blend these, you'll be building an original and innovative platform that will make you more excited and fulfilled than you ever thought possible.

The Perfect Writing Career Is like a Comfortable Shoe

Forcing yourself into a writing career that doesn't reflect your own personal talents and skills is like trying to wear a shoe that doesn't fit. You'll only come away with blisters.

It may go something like this. You were told to blog, so you're blogging, but you're short on topics to blog about. Or maybe you're getting few readers. You were told to get on social media to sell books, but it's not helping and you're wondering why. You worked hard for a traditional publishing contract and you finally got it, but when the book came out, it went unnoticed.

I could give you a hundred more examples. Chances are you set out on this writing path dreaming of bestsellers and oodles of time to pen them, but soon got lost in the foggy world of publishing and didn't know how to find your way forward again. You reached out for help. You learned about marketing and tried to apply what you learned. You took this and that tributary, not knowing if they would be the best way for *you*—all while feeling filled with self-doubt and fear and wondering if you were really going the right direction. Maybe things got better for a while and the sun peeked out, but then the fog returned. The bottom line is, you've worked hard, but in the end, it seems like no one is paying any attention.

I'm here to help you find a path out of the fog, into the sun and on up your mountain of success. All I ask is that you think about things a little differently.

Steps to Your Own Unique Writing Career

As we move forward, I'm going to help you to:

   a.   learn what your strengths are as a writer and a person,

b. use those strengths to explore new ways to build your own unique career, and

c. watch for the subtle signs along the way that will point you where you need to go.

Those days of running around doing what you think you should be doing, or whatever this or that person said you should do to have a successful writing career, are over. Instead, you will start zeroing in on your own niche and building *your own career*. Just watch—your days are about to become much more exciting, challenging, and fun.

CHAPTER 2

WHAT YOU REALLY WANT FROM WRITING

O NE SUMMER I attended a literary panel discussion featuring award-winning, bestselling writers. The experience was outstanding in many ways, but I was surprised by what one author had to say. This author had been lauded over and over again for his talents and had been compared to Dostoyevsky. He'd also won numerous awards for his fiction, including international prizes and the PEN/Hemingway award.

When asked how all this had affected him, he just shrugged, shook his head, and gave us a blank expression. In a calm voice, he described receiving "the call" for each award and told us how excited he had been, every time expecting his life would change, but within a few weeks, realizing things had stayed pretty much the same. I imagined all the writers in the audience were thinking the same thing: *If after all that nothing changes, then what?*

Most writers dream of what this man had—work that was admired by all the powers that be in the literary world, groups extending invitations to speak on elevated panels with other accomplished authors, young talents looking to him for advice, and book lovers waiting with bated breath for his next release. But none of us attending that day considered the idea that should all our dreams come true, nothing in our lives would really change. How could that be?

Writing One or Two Books Is Unlikely to Create a Full-Time Salary

One of the biggest myths about being a writer is that if you write the right book, you'll be financially set for life. According to the *Digital Book World/Writer's Digest* 2014 survey of over 9,200 writers, most who were self-published or hybrid (both self-published and traditionally published), earned only $1–999 per year. Only between 5–10 percent of hybrid authors made over $100,000 per year, and among traditionally published authors, only 2 percent made over $100,000 per year from their writing.

"One of the biggest myths about becoming a successful novelist," wrote Ros Barber, winner of the Desmond Elliott Prize for fiction, in her blog entitled *Authors and the Truth About Money*, "is that it means you're rolling in it." She went on to explain that even though she received a "handsome advance" for her first novel, *The Marlowe Papers*, that advance was for four years' work and was paid out over the next two years, and was further diminished by agent's fees and taxes.

To make ends meet, Barber got a job as a creative writing lecturer at the University of London, but teaching two-and-a-half days a week meant she earned only half a salary, so she had to come up with other ways to make money and manage expenses. Although she bemoaned the fact that this lifestyle interfered with her writing time, she concluded with this:

"It is clear that authors, like other creative people looking to make a living doing what they love and are good at (bringing joy to many people in the process), are going to have to look to new ways of supporting themselves."

Ask most any experienced author and you'll hear a similar story. The question then becomes: Is it worth it to risk your time, talent, and well-being to chase a dream that is unlikely to come true? I say you can still enjoy the payoff you're looking for if you shift your goals just a little bit.

Don't Work Your Tail off for What You "Think" You Want

Many writers work their tails off to achieve what they thought they wanted—a traditional publishing contract, a place on the bestseller list, awards, money in the bank—only to find out, usually years later, that what they thought would happen as a result of those achievements didn't happen.

This sort of outcome usually occurs because of one important reason: the writer's goals didn't line up with what he really wanted. This isn't a huge surprise, because even though you may "think" you know what you want as a writer, it takes significant introspection to identify your true goal.

Maybe you enjoy writing fiction, so your goal is to land a traditional publishing contract for a novel. Over a period of several years, you spend all your extra time writing, getting feedback, and rewriting, gradually getting better at your craft while holding high that dream of a traditional publishing contract.

Finally, the day comes when a publisher signs you on. You sail through the next year or two in book production, and feel on top of the world on publication day. Then, a year later, you realize your life hasn't changed like you thought it would. Your book got some good reviews and sold pretty well for a first novel, but you're still at the same job, in the same house, with the same people around you, and honestly, you don't feel much different than you did before the book was published. Of course, you've gained a sense of personal satisfaction, but if you're truly honest with yourself, you realize this is just not enough.

Determining What You Really Want from Your Writing Career

It's time to pull out your journal. I'm about to give you your first assignment. Let's try something fun. Start by thinking about the biggest goal you want to achieve through your writing, and then consider this question: If you achieve this goal, what do you hope it will bring you? If you're not sure, consider these examples: money, fame, respect, more time to write, lots of fans, the ability to quit your day job, validation of your talent, attention, peace of mind, etc.

If you achieve this goal, how do you
want it to change your life?

Write the answer in your journal.

Don't skip this step!

I'll give you some time…

Now consider that no matter what your answer was, it's likely your writing will *not* bring you this thing. There are exceptions, of course. If you wrote down that you hoped a traditional publishing contract might give you peace of mind, it's possible that will happen, at least temporarily. But in most cases, writers tend to want far too much from their craft. We all start out believing that if only we can get "good enough," then writing will solve all our problems, make life easier, bring us the confidence and positive attention we deserve, and even help us to be brighter, happier people. You probably haven't thought about these things consciously. These are feelings that tend to live in the back of your mind and heart, but if you dig deep enough, you'll find them. They're there, they're real, and they're motivating you. In fact, they're the reason you're doing what you're doing.

Is that a bad thing? Absolutely not! Whatever feelings you have about writing, you need to bring them out into the open where you can see them clearly and use them in a constructive way. The problem is not what you want from your writing—it's how you go about getting it.

Why Writers Want Writing Careers

Here are some examples of the why writers may want to build writing careers:

- They have a vision they want to share with others.

- They enjoy writing stories and want more time to do that without a day job interfering.

- They hope to make money with writing so they don't have to do other things they don't enjoy.

- They crave recognition and imagine glowing reviews and adoring readers.

- They want to live the life they imagine other successful writers living.

- They're responding to old hurts or past wounds and are driven by an emotional need to "show them."

- They're confident of their writing skills and "hope" they'll lead to success.

- They're creative individuals who long for different lives than the ones they have and hope writing books will help them change their current situations.

This is in no way meant to be an all-inclusive list, but it gives the most common reasons writers go after a writing career. The point is to show you that your reasons for pursuing a writing goal are universal and valid. Now that we've established that fact, it's time to burst that fantasy bubble with a bit of reality.

When Your Writing Life Doesn't Produce the Perfect Life

I've pursued the typical writing path, thinking it would bring me what I wanted, and been sorely disappointed. I've lived through that despair, and come out the other side realizing one thing: I knew what I wanted, but I didn't know how to get it.

I wanted a fulfilling, exciting writing career. I was happy to work hard, but I wanted to receive the rewards of that work. I wanted to feel that my efforts *meant* something. I wanted to connect with other people. I wanted to wake up each day knowing I had exciting projects waiting for me, and that my career was building, not stagnating.

These are not extraordinary things to ask for, and you may want some of these same things too. So let's get down to business so you can actually get that satisfaction you're craving from your writing career.

Find the Feeling

To discover what you *really* want from your writing, imagine how you want to *feel* as a successful writer. You already believe, sort of unconsciously, that reaching your goal will make you feel a certain way. You must identify that feeling.

It's too easy to get caught up in what we think we're *supposed* to do. We're supposed to blog, self-publish, or go after a traditional publishing contract, write at least one book a year, stay active on social media, etc. If you take a step back, though, and give yourself time to really dig deep into what you truly desire, it's possible to create a much more fulfilling career for yourself down the road—and that's definitely worth a few days of introspection, using the following exercises as your guide. Whatever you do, please don't skip these! This is a critical step in finding your niche, establishing your successful platform, and creating your perfect writing career.

Six Ways to Discover What You Really Want from Writing

1. Journal about it.

The best thing about a journal is that it's safe. Even if you're afraid to admit what you really want because you think it sounds selfish or shallow, in your journal, no one's judging. Here, you can be brutally honest about what you hope your writing career will bring you—financial security, recognition, pride in yourself, freedom, respect—whatever it is, you are free to write it here. Don't be surprised if you discover some things you didn't expect.

Now open your journal and answer this question:

> *In my heart of hearts, what do I really*
> *want from my writing right now?*

After you answer that question, then ask yourself:

> *Why do I want that?*

In response to that question, continue to ask "why" again and again until you discover the core desire that is fueling this goal of yours. Let me give you an example.

> *In my heart of hearts, what do I really*
> *want from my writing right now?*

I want a traditional publishing contract for my novel.

> *Why do I want that?*

I want the validation that my writing is good enough to be chosen by a traditional publisher.

> *Why do I want that?*

I want to feel like my writing is good enough.

> *Why do I want that?*

Because it makes me feel good if others think my writing is good.

Why?

Because if others think my writing is good, maybe they will think I'm good too.

Aha! Here we come to the core desire fueling this goal. Can you see it? The writer is hoping his writing will help him to feel better about himself. Now that he knows this, he can approach his goal from two different directions. Yes, he can continue to focus on improving his writing, but he can *also* focus on other ways to feel "good enough." The more he can find validation in other ways, the less pressure he puts on his writing to do it for him, and the happier he will be in his writing career.

Let's try another example.

In my heart of hearts, what do I really
want from my writing right now?

I want to sell a lot of books.

Why do I want that?

I want to earn money from my writing.

Why do I want that?

I'd like to earn money doing something I enjoy doing.

Why do I want that?

Because I'm tired of doing things I don't like to do to earn money.

Why?

Because some days I don't know if I can keep doing it anymore.

Aha! We've come to the core of the issue here—this writer is burned out and exhausted from the other work she's doing. Once she can identify this core feeling, she can approach her goal from two directions. One, she can focus on finding writing projects that have the best odds of making money (i.e., freelance writing, ghostwriting, nonfiction writing), and two, she can see if she can ease the pressure on herself at her other job. Perhaps she needs to update her resume and start looking for new employment even while she's working on her writing, so she's not putting all the pressure to earn money on her writing alone.

See how this works? If you dig down deep enough to find out what's really going on in your psyche, you can then gain clarity on what you're really looking for, and increase your odds that you'll actually be able to find it. Often writers expect their writing to solve all their problems, which is a recipe for failure because there's no way writing can do all that for you. Instead, identify what you really need, then find multiple ways to fulfill that need, and you're likely to experience more success in your writing career.

Instead of this ...	think this.
I have to get that traditional publishing contract so I'll feel good enough.	I'll keep trying for that traditional publishing contract, but meanwhile I'll work on feeling "good enough" in other ways too.
I have to sell lots of books so I can quit my day job.	I'll work at creating a great marketing plan for my books, but I'll also see if I can find other work that feels more satisfying.
I have to win an award so my family respects my writing time.	I'll continue to enter my work into contests, but meanwhile I'll create boundaries around my writing time that I won't allow family members to cross.
I have to succeed at writing so I won't feel like such a failure.	I'll keep working on my writing, but I'll also start focusing on my strengths as a person, and look for other ways to develop my skills.

2. Pinpoint the disappointment.

Do you have a general sense of disappointment about your writing career? If someone asked you what you were disappointed by, would you be able to put it into words? Let's try. Using your journal, complete the following sentences.

    a. I'm disappointed that ...

    b. That disappointed me because I wanted ...

    c. I wanted that because ...

    d. I thought once I had that, I would feel ...

    e. I wanted to feel that way because ...

Once you've completed all these sentences, you should have a pretty good idea of what you really wanted. Now you can start to think of new ways you may be able to get it.

3. Recall the rewarding experiences.

No matter how your career has gone so far, it's likely you've had at least a few rewarding experiences. Maybe it was when your agent talked about your novel in a way that made it plain she *got it*. Maybe it was reading your story to a group of kids. Maybe it was running a workshop about a topic you're passionate about. Write down three rewarding experiences that come to mind:

a. Rewarding experience #1:
b. Rewarding experience #2:
c. Rewarding experience #3:

Recalling these experiences can help you identify what you really want—to have someone understand what you write, to share your stories with youngsters, or to help inspire and uplift others. Knowing that, you can renew your efforts to connect with like-minded people, perhaps through a niche blog, by writing smaller pieces for publications that fit your vision, or by taking your ideas out to speaking events. Voilà—just by focusing on what you really want from writing, you're suddenly thinking about activities that will expand your platform!

The options are endless once you know what really makes your heart sing. Spend some time recalling each moment in your writing career that gave you a feeling of true joy, and then look them all over and find out what they have in common. Why were they so enjoyable? Answer that question and you'll gain insight into what you're really looking for.

4. Pen your writer's obituary.

This exercise can be a fun and creative way to figure out exactly what you want from your writing career. You just have to follow two rules. First, you can't include anything in your obituary that you can't control. In other words, no "Marie was a Pulitzer Prize-winning author…" (unless you actually *are* a Pulitzer Prize winner). You can't control whether you win the Pulitzer Prize, and this obituary is only about what you can control.

Second, this obituary must be only about your writing and creative career. So don't talk about your beloved pets or how you enjoyed skiing. Focus solely on how you would like to be remembered as a writer and creative person.

You can follow the formula below, or create your own. I've skipped some of the normal obituary formalities ("survived by," "was born in," and the like) to get right to the heart of the exercise—your writing career.

_____ (name) died

_____ (unexpectedly/peacefully) in

_____ (location) on _____ (date) in

_____ (city, state) at the age of _____ (age).

_____ (first name) began _____ (his/her) career as a writer and creative entrepreneur on _____ (date). Over _____ (period of time), _____ (he/she) grew that career into a thriving business, creating _____

(work), _____ (projects), and
_____ (other). The people _____ (he/
she) touched with _____ (his/her) work remember _____ (him/
her) as a _____ (characteristic) artist who
_____ (action; i.e., encouraged them to
pursue their goals, inspired them to X, motivated them to Y,
touched them in Z ways, taught them X, etc.).

_____ (name) was accomplished
at _____ (skill/talent) and often
_____ (example of talent and/or strength).
_____(He/she) was a _____ (characteristic;
e.g. generous, witty, dedicated, conscientious, caring, etc.) individual who loved _____ (subject—what you
write about or the main interest reflected in your writing) and who
was passionate about _____ (passion; e.g.,
changing X about Y, educating Z, sharing her travel adventures,
exploring relationships, designing airplanes and spaceships, etc.).
_____ (He/she) often _____ (did what?) to
_____ (help whom?).

A funeral is scheduled for _____(time and
date) at _____(location), with a reception to follow at _____(location). The
theme of the reception is _____ (reflec-
tive of your work), and all are invited to dress up and celebrate
_____(name)'s life and creative work.
In lieu of flowers, please send _____

(what?—maybe something that fits in with your life's work) to
_____ (place or person).

5. Pretend to be your own fan.

In this exercise, you're going to put on your writer's hat and pretend you're a specific character—one of your own fans. If you don't have fans yet, it's okay, it doesn't matter. Even if you do, it might be best to avoid thinking about real people for the moment, as what you want to do is imagine your *ideal* fan. This is the person who loves what you do and how you do it in your best imaginary world. To this person, you are someone he or she wants to emulate. You are the shining star leading the way.

With that in mind, fill out the following statement as your devoted fan would by inserting words that best describe how you want to be known as an author and creative business owner. Get into the role—imagine you are this fan and you're inspired by this author (you) and his/her work. Be sure to use your name and feel free to speak about yourself in the third person. You want to gain some distance—that is the point of this exercise—so imagine when you're talking about yourself that you're actually talking about another person (one you like).

Fan Statement

I'm so excited! Next weekend, I'm going to meet _____ (author name—you). _____ (He's/she's) going to be _____ (activity, i.e. signing books, speaking, reading, teaching, etc.) at _____ (event—whatever event you imagine yourself participating in) and I'm going! I'm thrilled because _____ (he/she) has inspired me through (his/her)_____ (books, workshops, blog, etc.) to always _____ (something related to your author theme, or something you'd like to inspire others to do). _____ (His/Her) work is so _____ (adjective describing your work) and _____ (another adjective) that it always makes me feel _____ (how you want your readers/fans to feel).

I hope I get a chance to talk to _____ (him/her) and let _____ (him/her) know how much _____ (he's/she's) helped me. Because of _____ (him/her), I feel more _____ (how you want readers to feel) about _____ (topic or subject). Plus _____ (he/she) is just so _____ (characteristic you want to be known for; i.e., inspiring, motivating, exciting, energizing, knowledgeable, creative, caring, dynamic, helpful, etc.)!

6. Define the hardships you're willing to endure.

Most of the time when you think about what you want to get out of your writing career, you probably think about the positive possibilities, such as:

- Being able to write and have people enjoy what you write

- Making a little money on the side or even making a living doing what you love

- Gaining some recognition for your creative talent

- Moving other people to take action

- Helping or inspiring other people through your creative work

- Building expertise in an area you're passionate about

For this exercise, it's time to think about the other side of the coin—what pain you're willing to endure to reach your goals. It's easy to imagine great success, raving fans, money pouring in, and that moment when you waltz into your boss's office and quit your day job. We'd all love to have those experiences, and on the surface, it seems there's nothing wrong with dreaming about them. These imaginings can lead you down the wrong road, though, if you fail to consider what it's going to take to make those sorts of dreams come true.

None of that stuff is going to come your way without a lot of hard work. Talk to any author who's "made it." And when I say made it, I mean she's published several books, she has readers who enjoy her work, she's established a creative business she loves, and she's making some money from her efforts. She's built up a "tribe" of her own who knows and respects her, and looks forward to supporting whatever she does next.

Never doubt it: that author had to sweat blood and tears to get where she is. She had to put in countless hours that were never reimbursed. She had to go through months or even years scraping by so she could invest in herself and her business. She had to survive periods of discouragement and possibly burnout and recover and start again. She had to overcome self-doubt, risk making mistakes, fail and fail again, endure the humiliation of difficult critiques or bad reviews, and perhaps even stand up in the face of family and friends who questioned what she was "wasting her time" on. Through all those hours and days and weeks and years she was doing all that, she had to believe somewhere deep down inside of her that it would all be worth it in the end.

What pain are you willing to endure to make your dreams of

owning a thriving writing or creative business come true? Discovering the answer to that question can help you determine how much you really want to reach your goals, and may also help you prioritize which ones are worth the effort you'll have to put in.

Pain Endurance Quiz

Below, answer each question with a number from one to ten, with one representing "not willing" and ten representing "definitely willing." I'm willing to endure:

1. _____ Financial pain (finances are tight, live frugally or cut back)

2. _____ Emotional pain (self-doubt, discouragement, depressed feelings)

3. _____ Mental pain (working insane hours, burnout, confusion)

4. _____ Physical pain (fatigue, headaches, aches and pains)

5. _____ Leisure pain (less time/money for fun, going out, going on vacation)

6. _____ Drudgery pain (doing things you don't enjoy, like paper work, taxes, organization tasks, website updates, learning something new that's boring)

7. _____ Decision pain (total responsibility for outcomes, pressured to make the right decisions, disappointment when making mistakes)

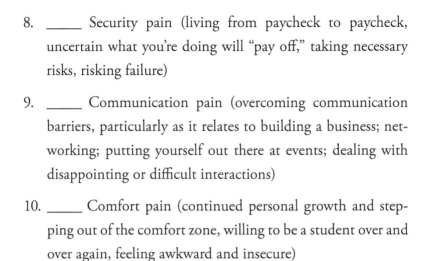

8. _____ Security pain (living from paycheck to paycheck, uncertain what you're doing will "pay off," taking necessary risks, risking failure)

9. _____ Communication pain (overcoming communication barriers, particularly as it relates to building a business; networking; putting yourself out there at events; dealing with disappointing or difficult interactions)

10. _____ Comfort pain (continued personal growth and stepping out of the comfort zone, willing to be a student over and over again, feeling awkward and insecure)

Now examine your answers. If you're willing to endure all these potentially painful situations, then good for you—you just increased your odds of success. If you're only willing to endure some of them, it's time to modify your goals to work within your limits.

If you're not willing to endure financial pain, for example, then you have to realize you may need to keep your day job for the long term. You may miss out on important learning opportunities (writing workshops, critiques), you may be unable to create a website that looks as professional as you'd like, or your self-published book may not meet your high quality standard, the latter two of which typically take substantial investments.

Because of these factors, it may take you longer to reach your goals than you'd like. There's nothing wrong with that—many writers have to modify this one because they're raising a family, for instance, or they're acting as caregivers. The important thing is to realize what you can't endure right now so you can adjust your expectations accordingly and maintain your motivation.

If you're not willing to endure physical pain, you need to be sure you put into place lifestyle habits that will help prevent injury. I consistently recommend doing that on my motivational website *Writing and Wellness* (www.writingandwellness.com) because it's so easy for writers to hurt themselves the way they physically work. Hours sitting or even standing at the computer can be detrimental to your health, and you'd be more productive and efficient if you took the time to eat a healthy diet and exercise every day.

It helps if you know yourself. If you are a highly sensitive person, for example, you may have to suffer from headaches or other aches and pains when performing tasks related to your business. Many writers, for example, suffer physically when going to conferences, simply because all the interaction—though stimulating and exciting—wears them out. Me personally, I occasionally suffer from headaches when speaking at conferences because I usually don't sleep well in a hotel the night before, and lack of sleep is a prominent migraine trigger. I'm willing to endure that physical pain because I love helping other writers to succeed.

In many of the categories above, you can modify your approach to how you run your business and your life to reduce your risk. It's worthwhile to try, but realize at some point, and perhaps more often than you'd like, you must tolerate some uncomfortable challenges.

What pain are you willing to endure? Remember—it's easy to be in love with the idea of running your own creative business, earning money on the side, and gaining positive recognition for your work. Anyone can do that, and a lot of people do—they dream of a life like that. But have you noticed how many just keep dreaming but never make those dreams come true?

There's a reason for that—they aren't willing to make the necessary sacrifices. You have to ask yourself now: "What am I willing to give up or endure to make my dream come true?"

Start Thinking about Your Author Platform

Now that you've learned a little more about yourself and what you're looking for in your writing, it's time to talk more seriously about platform. No doubt you've heard that word somewhere along the way, or maybe you've already spent years building yours. In the next chapter, I'll help you see why your platform, instead of being something you *have* to do to sell your books, can be *the key* to growing your writing and creative business.

CHAPTER 3

HOW AN AUTHOR PLATFORM SAVES YOU

Y*OU NEED AN author platform,* they said. *What's that?* you asked. You got several answers. *Your visibility,* they said. *Your ability to sell books. Your reach as an author. Your connections. Who you are. Media outlets you can use to increase awareness of your releases and other activities.*

It can be confusing to talk about platform, so let me simplify it. I prefer writer and publishing industry specialist Jane Friedman's definition. She wrote on her blog, *Jane Friedman,* that an author platform is your "ability to sell books because of who you are or who you can reach." In other words, your ability to attract readers.

No matter what else you may want from writing, I'm quite sure that you—like most writers—want readers. (If you're a freelance writer or editor, you may want clients more than readers, but if you can attract more readers to your platform, you're more likely to attract more clients, too.) Perhaps you would still write even if no one ever read your work, but your chances of becoming a better writer and living up to your potential are much greater if you can build your readership.

It's the same with any art. Imagine a musician. He spends months in the studio writing and recording, but then what? He goes out and shares his music with an audience. He fulfills his purpose by playing for others, and as he does so, he receives their feedback. He learns what they do and don't respond to, and when he returns to the studio, he can't help but allow that feedback to shape his next project. With an audience, he grows and becomes more the artist he was meant to be.

The same thing happens with a painter. She spends months or maybe years painting all by herself, but then what? She takes her paintings to a gallery, or she puts them on a website, or she somehow gets her work out into the world. She wants it to be seen—needs it to be seen, needs to hear what viewers think about her art. Then she can use that support to go back and create more.

Writers also need readers to complete the creative cycle. The problem is, readers are more difficult to find today than ever before. The market is flooded with blogs, stories, books, poems, and articles. Self-publishing has opened the floodgates, and now we have way more books than we have people who want to read them. Supply has outpaced demand, which means writers often struggle to find their own tribe of readers.

You may think the answer lies in marketing, and yes, if you become proficient at marketing, you do have a better chance of success, but that takes time and skill, and in the end, won't necessarily get you the results you want. I know writers who have spent thousands on publicity, ads, tours, and more, never to recoup their investments. If you're not worried about money, that's not really a problem, but most writers do have limited budgets to work with.

And then what if you don't enjoy marketing? What if you find that it feels hollow and draining, sapping energy from you rather than giving energy back?

The Genius of the Author Platform

Writing and publishing a book, or even two or three books, won't automatically get you readers. It can happen, particularly in the romance, mystery, and thriller genres, and often in the science fiction and fantasy ones too. But writers who manage it are usually fast writers, putting out a couple books or more per year and have also mastered marketing. It takes time, energy, and self-education, which can be tough if you have a day job and a family to take care of. In the end, most writers need more than just "the books" to bring readers their way.

You can look at this as a negative effect of the modern world or you can look at it as a way to broaden your career. With a robust author platform, you not only have a more direct line to your readers, you also have a living, breathing machine into which you can continue to pour your creative efforts all while growing, learning, and expanding your skills.

Let me give you an example. For years, I toiled away on my stories and then my novels without much feedback. I got the occasional encouraging note from an editor or agent and once in a while a promising contest critique, but I worked largely alone and without readers. It was when I got my first publishing contract that I was introduced to the whole concept of building a platform, and so set to creating a website and blog. My first efforts weren't bad, but the blog didn't attract the readers I hoped for. Still, I maintained it for a couple years until shortly before I got my second publishing contract.

Then I had a new idea to combine the focus of my day job—health writing—with my love of creative writing.

I sketched out what the new site would look like and pitched the idea to supportive friends. Within a few months, *Writing and Wellness* was born. It grew quickly, and with it the knowledge that I had finally found my "niche" in the blogging world. I had also found a way to broaden my reach and attract the readers I'd been looking for, as well as expand my writing career as a whole.

Suddenly I was writing new books for my audience, guest posting with topics in my niche, creating a community, conducting workshops, speaking at conferences, and becoming recognized as an expert in my niche, all while feeling more energized and motivated than I ever had in the past. The fact that I had to build an author platform to support my books helped expand my writing career in a way I never would have dreamed of when I was first starting out.

You, too, can find your niche in the writing world, and I think you'll agree it's a lot better option than just trying to "sell" your books. The problem with marketing is that it seems like we're constantly asking people to, "Please buy my book!" Not only do we request support on our social media feeds, we also tend to become pests around friends and family. "Oh, I wrote about that in my book. Have you read it? Here's a copy!" We go to conferences and at every opportunity, brag about our publications. Yet this sort of approach turns more people away than it attracts.

Your Author Platform Creates Purpose

Your author platform is the perfect tool to attract readers. It may include a website, blog, guest posts on other blogs, and a social media presence. You may also choose to add a YouTube channel and/or a podcast, public speaking events, online workshops, magazine or journal articles, writing or reading retreats, ghostwriting and editing, and other services, all depending on your unique strengths and skills.

The more you can offer your reader, the more you have to draw from to shape your platform until at some point, it evolves to naturally showcase a deeper purpose you may not have even considered before.

Maryanne Pope, a writer from Vancouver Island that I featured on *Writing and Wellness*, had wanted to write a book for years, but she never got around to it. Then tragedy struck:

> On Thursday, September 28th, 2000, my husband John and I had an argument while walking our dog. I told him how scared I was of waking up twenty years later and still not having finished writing a book. John stopped walking, turned to me, and said, "You're probably right about that, Maryanne. Just as long as you know that will have been your choice."
>
> Ouch. But he was right. By that point, we'd been together as a couple for twelve years … that's a long time listening to someone talk about wanting to become a writer—and complaining about how she doesn't have the time or money—yet doing little in the way of any actual writing.
>
> After John went to work that night—he was a police officer—I promised myself I would wake up early the next morning and do an hour of writing before going to my clerical job. *I'll show him!* I thought. But when my alarm clock went off the next morning, I pushed snooze: *I'm too tired. I don't want to get up.*

And wouldn't you know it, at the exact same time I was pushing snooze yet again on my writing dream, John was dying on the lunchroom floor of a warehouse. He had been investigating a breaking-and-entering complaint and was searching the mezzanine level when he stepped from a safe surface right through an unmarked false ceiling. There was no safety railing in place to warn him—or anyone else— about the danger. He fell a mere nine feet into the lunchroom below, but the back of his head struck the concrete with such force that he succumbed to a massive brain injury within hours. He was 32. So was I.

The complaint turned out to be a false alarm; there had been no intruder in the building. My wake-up call, however, was devastatingly real. Two weeks later, I started writing what would become my creative nonfiction book, *A Widow's Awakening*. It took me eight years to get the manuscript— and me—where it needed to be. But I did it.

Maryanne not only wrote her book, she also found new purpose in the writing:

Writing, of course, was not the only thing I had to contend with in the wake of John's easily preventable death. In addition to the myriad of practical matters that needed to be sorted—figuring out my new (and unwanted) life while managing dozens of loved ones who were concerned about me (to this day, I still wince when the phone rings)—there was also a rather large elephant in the living room to contend with: the issue that led to John's death … an unsafe workplace.

And so, onto my already seriously overloaded plate, I placed the responsibility (some might say burden) of also becoming a workplace safety advocate. Thankfully, I wasn't alone in this endeavor.

After John's death, several of his police recruit classmates started the John Petropoulos Memorial Fund (JPMF), which is now a charity that educates the public about why and how to ensure their workplace is safe for everyone, including first responders. Over the years, the JPMF has produced five TV ads that have aired over a million times, as well as a ten-minute safety video that is viewed online and shown in presentations.

I put my heart and soul—and time and money—into working with other like-minded people to raise awareness about workplace safety, so that others don't have to go through what I did ... nor have their lives cut drastically short, as did John.

To this day, Maryanne devotes 20 percent of her book sales to JPMF and gives presentations about workplace safety and living with loss to a variety of organizations. She continues to use her writing voice to support this cause that is near and dear to her heart, and as she has broadened her reader base through these activities, she's also been able to broaden her creative pursuits.

You can see in Maryanne's story how finding a purpose for her writing—increasing awareness about workplace safety, sharing her own loss and grief, and helping others through theirs—gave her not only an author platform that attracted readers, but a true reason to keep writing regardless of critiques, reviews, sales, and the rest. We all need something like this—a deeper, bigger reason to do what we do. It sustains us and provides a place where we can regularly rekindle our energy, passion, and motivation.

Sometimes You Find Purpose in Unique Ways

Angelique L'Amour, daughter of famous writer Louis L'Amour, had always been a writer. She started keeping a journal at the age of seven and continued to write "for fun" after that. She drifted away from journaling as an adult, but then she was diagnosed with cancer in 2009. After that, she wrote, "my journaling came rushing back as my closest ally. It was in a different form, however. Instead of the notebooks I always carried, I began a blog called *My Story Right Now.*"

In that blog, Angelique wrote about her experiences raising two girls and going through cancer treatments at the same time. "That year both our daughters were playing on soccer teams, doing theater, and going to school, and I was teaching Creative Writing and Literature at a local Catholic School. Needless to say, I was busy."

Adding cancer surgeries and treatment to the mix along with frequently feeling lousy made it all the more difficult. "I was exhausted, but I got through each week keeping our family moving forward and without our entire lives becoming my cancer treatment. And the people I heard from wanted to know how I did it. The blog began as a way to communicate with my family about my life and keep my mom and husband from constantly having to answer the same questions. It grew into a place where many people went for help, advice, and guidance … "

Her blog grew, and so did her rewards. "I got encouraged by feedback. People sent emails or commented or told me in person that I was a light, I had an amazing attitude, and they all wished they could be the way I was. That encouraged me."

When her intuition led to writing a book, the *Chemo Cupcakes and Carpools* trilogy was born—a guide for parents navigating the coexisting worlds of cancer treatment and parenting. Angelique had naturally expanded her platform. When I met her at a writer's conference in Dallas-Fort Worth, she was speaking about managing emotions in writing and told her story of writing through cancer treatments. I found her to be inspiring and learned that after finishing the *Chemo Cupcakes and Carpools* trilogy, she not only continued to write fiction, but started working on a new spiritual book, all with her readers in mind. "I have to keep moving forward so that I can finish and help more people when they are going through something."

These are the words of a writer who has found her platform—a writer who feels purpose in what she's doing.

A Platform Saves a Writer during Troubled Times

Sandy Fussell's career was sailing along successfully. A writer with a natural love for young people, she was enjoying a thriving platform that included speaking in schools, helping students learn more about writing, developing resources for teachers, and serving as in-schools Literary Festival Coordinator at The Story Crowd. She released book after book, and everything was going great until tragedy hit home.

"My biggest emotional challenge was watching a writing career that had started successfully slowly fade away due to circumstances outside my control," she wrote in her feature on *Writing and Wellness*. "I was achieving everything I planned. I called myself the Cinderella Writer, and I'd laughingly say I was worried I might turn into a pumpkin. The 'pumpkin years' did come but not in the way

I expected. My youngest son developed a painful, chronic medical condition. For the past six years, I've been a stay-at-home caregiver and tutor. During this time, I also survived three life-threatening illnesses of my own, including a rare cancer."

Sandy's illness and her son's health challenges severely impacted her writing career.

"Time to write was so meager, fractured, and emotionally stressed," she said, "even I could see everything I produced was awful. This year my son is coping better and new medical options are providing hope. I'm writing freely once more. It's like starting all over again."

What saved Sandy during those difficult years was her writing platform. "It was hard to withdraw from successfully doing what I loved, but eventually I was too tired, too sad, and too worried about my son to write in the windows of time that came my way. With family support, I focused instead on social media, workshops, and school visits, which kept my writer profile active. Kids and their teachers and librarians are particularly wonderful for inspiration and motivation. They made me feel like I was still an author, even if there wasn't a new book in sight. That helped me get through the tough times."

I'm happy to say that both Sandy and her son are doing better now, and Sandy is back to writing, but it was because of her established platform that she didn't disappear from readers' minds while she was dealing with her health issues. She adds, "My favorite writing quote is from Isaac Asimov: 'I write for the same reason I breathe.' This is true for me, too, and I will always keep writing, no matter what obstacles are flung at me. But it's also true I want to write for readers, not just myself. My writing feels incomplete otherwise."

Discover More: Your Author Platform

It takes time and exploration to find an author platform that works for you. Maybe you already have one. If so, your next step is to make it as robust and attractive to readers as possible. If you don't have one, or if the one you have doesn't feel "right" for whatever reason, don't worry—the more you work through this book, the more clues you'll find about discovering your niche and using it to get noticed.

I hope you're beginning to see the many ways you can expand your career, use your strengths to your advantage, and reach the people who are interested in what you're doing. That's what a platform is—your way to catch people's attention. From there, you can take new actions to help establish a strong base to support you as you continue to create.

To dive deeper into your author platform—and to start zeroing in on your unique creative niche—use your journal or notebook to answer the following four questions.

1. I felt happiest when a reader told me that my story _____. (Examples may include: "excited her, made her cry, made her think, scared her.")

2. The most valuable compliment I ever got on my writing was when _____. (This doesn't have to refer specifically to a book—it could be on any writing you've ever done.)

3. When I'm writing a story, what I really hope to do is make the reader _____. (Examples may include: "change his mind, feel better about himself, feel an emotion [be specific], take action, fall in love with my characters, laugh, feel like he's visited new locations.")

4. The themes that appear over and over again in my writing are _____. (Examples may include: "love is always worth it, good triumphs evil, life isn't how it appears, you have to be strong to survive, loss is transforming, laughter is necessary.")

Now review your answers to see if they have anything in common. If they do, chances are you will see a possible niche start to reveal itself. Continue to brainstorm for a few minutes, and write down your observations. Don't try to edit them at this point. You will keep building on these ideas and refer back to them in the coming chapters. Gradually, you'll gather the tools you need to create your career as a successful writer with a loyal following.

CHAPTER 4

USE MOTIVATION TO FIND YOUR TRUTH NORTH

G ETTING A SUCCESSFUL writing career off the ground requires a large amount of personal discovery. You have to find out what's going to work best for you and the types of writing you create. Every writer is unique, and there is more than one way to reach success. You do, however, have to plot your own path, and that can be frightening because it means you will probably make your fair share of mistakes. Fear of failure is often the reason why we look to others for direction when what we need to do is face the fear, take the time and effort required to discover our own strengths and passions, and then summon the courage to strike out on our own.

The biggest mistake I made early on was failing to dig deep enough into my own psyche to figure out the type of writing career that could really work for me. Instead, I took the simple route and made a number of mistakes based on incorrect assumptions including:

1. If only I could get a publishing contract, my writing career would take off.

2. If I wrote a story a publisher deemed good enough to publish, they would take care of the rest, including marketing and sales.

3. The only thing I needed to concentrate on was writing and becoming a better writer.

The first two assumptions were flat-out wrong, and the third only partially right. In fact, I've thought many times, if I'd known then what I know now, I could have gotten started on a "real" writing career long before I did. Instead, I spent over a decade floundering and battling the demons of self-doubt and discouragement, simply because I was following the wrong path.

If you find yourself in a similar place right now, think seriously about this: If you're not experiencing the rewarding, successful writing career you hoped for, it may be that you've lost your way.

Getting lost happens when traveling in your car as well as through your life. The difference is if you end up driving on the wrong road in the middle of nowhere, you may get a little irritated, but most likely, you'll turn around, go back to a familiar place, and start over. You won't waste time doubting your ability to drive or navigate, so don't do that in your writing career. When things don't go the way you thought they would, don't blame your writing or your perceived lack of talent or ability, or heaven forbid, doubt if you should be writing at all!

Yes, we all have room for improvement. And yes, a large part of becoming a successful writer is learning to write well. That's a given. But from my experience, a lot of good writers get stuck banging their heads against a wall not knowing what to do next when it comes to finding the success they crave. If you're a writer who's worked hard on improving the quality of your writing only to feel like it hasn't made much of a difference, you need to think about the road you're on and why you're on it.

Quiz

Considering where you are right now in your career, answer the following questions. If more than one answer appeals to you, choose the one that resembles how you feel or act *most* of the time.

1. Why are you going after the main goal you're chasing?

a. I've seen bestselling writers do it and succeed, so I'm trying to do it.

b. A high school or college teacher, or other writing mentor I admired told me to.

c. I want my own creative career and I think this is the way to get it.

d. I believe if I achieve this goal, I'll feel a sense of peace and accomplishment.

e. I'm responding to wrongs I've seen in the world that I want to make right.

2. When you get a rejection or experience another setback, how do you decide what to do next?

a. I read blogs/articles/books from writing experts and follow their directions.

b. I do what my writer's group suggests or what my writing friends think I should do.

   c. I think about it, decide what I want to do, and do that, no matter what other people say.

   d. I meditate or find another way to center myself, then let my intuition guide me.

   e. I imagine what I can do to make my project more impressive to others.

3. When you think about your future as a writer, what do you think about?

   a. Bestseller lists, contest wins, and book signings.

   b. Doing something my family and loved ones will be proud of.

   c. Making my mark in my own way and attaining more creative freedom.

   d. Finding creative fulfillment in my life.

   e. Using my work to change the way people think.

4. What do you take away from a writer's conference or workshop?

   a. I try to do exactly what the experts at the conference said to do.

   b. I stay connected with my new writer friends and regularly check in with how they're doing.

   c. I try to put into practice what I learned, but I usually end up doing things my way.

   d. I use the information that I sense in my gut will work for me, and discard the rest.

   e. I find a way to share what I've learned—with a writing group, social media group, or other.

5. So far in your writing career, what has impacted you the most?

    a. Seeing my byline in a journal or magazine, placing in a contest, or having my book published.

    b. Having my family and friends congratulate me on a writing achievement.

    c. Being able to do things the way I want to do them.

    d. Feeling like my work had meaning beyond just writing a story.

    e. Helping others to better understand issues that matter to me.

6. Which of the following frustrates you the most?

    a. When I get a rejection.

    b. When my family, friends, and/or writing friends don't read what I wrote.

    c. When I have to do something not of my choosing during my writing time.

    d. When my life gets so busy that I find it hard to "zone out" or get into my creative flow.

    e. When other people don't pay attention to the message I'm sending.

7. You'll feel you've reached the pinnacle of your writing career when:

    a. I make the bestseller list or win the Nobel Prize or something similar.

    b. My writing projects allow me to establish meaningful connections with other people.

c. I can write what I want when I want and not have to worry about what other people think.

d. I feel like I'm becoming the artist I sensed I was.

e. My readers and fans start to listen to my truth and take action based on what I advise.

8. I feel most discouraged about my writing when:

a. I fail to get that publishing contract or contest win I hoped for.

b. The people I care about don't seem to respond well to my writing.

c. I have to give up my writing time for other responsibilities.

d. My writing starts to feel rote and formulaic, and I lose my creative mojo.

e. No one seems to pay attention to what I have to say.

9. When you get a writing critique, what sort of praise makes you most proud?

a. When the critique says that I'm an accomplished writer.

b. When the reader responds to the relationships between the characters.

c. When the critique suggests I have a strong writing voice and to trust it more.

d. When the reader seems to "get" the subtler meanings in the book.

e. When the reader states that the book influenced his or her thinking about a subject.

10. When you're eighty years old and look back on your writing life, you'll feel at peace if:

    a. I receive the recognition I've worked so hard for.

    b. I have readers looking forward to my next book.

    c. I had the freedom to pursue the type of writing career I wanted.

    d. I learned more about myself, humankind, and life in general through my writing.

    e. People seemed to benefit and improve because of the work I did.

Scoring:

Now tally your results. How many: As_____ Bs_____ Cs_____ Ds_____ Es_____?

There are no right or wrong answers here, only those that reflect your true motivations. Which letter has the highest number of answers? Write that down, then check below to see what your results mean.

Mostly As: You're highly driven to achieve and you enjoy a challenge. You have a deep personal need to accomplish your goals, and are looking to reach your "personal best." You love opportunities that give you a chance to "win." You are motivated by **achievement** and **recognition**.

Mostly Bs: You want to please others with your accomplishments. It's important to you to have your friends, family, and writing mentors be proud of your work. You want to share and connect with others through what you're doing. You are motivated by **connection** and **relationships**.

Mostly Cs: You don't typically listen to advice from others and prefer to go your own way. You like being in control of your career and deciding for yourself what projects you will work on. You are motivated by **independence** and **freedom**.

Mostly Ds: You rely on your intuition to guide you, and you make decisions based on what you feel in your gut. Even when a project doesn't bring you the rewards you'd hoped for, you still enjoy the process of doing it. You are motivated by **creative fulfillment** and **transcendence**.

Mostly Es: You are interested in persuading others to think and do as you do—what you believe is right. You seek to change human behavior through your words and to make the world a better place. You are motivated by **influence** and **power**.

Based on your results, write down your answer to this question: I'm motivated by ... (If you ended up with the same number of responses in more than one group, choose which one seems most dominant to you when considering what motivates you to create.)

Take a few minutes to mull over your answer so it gets you thinking about two important points:

1. Why you're going in this particular direction.

2. What's motivating you to stay on this road.

These are the two critical details you need to know about yourself as a writer sooner rather than later because …

Motivation Drives Success

When you think about why you're doing what you're doing, it forces you to take a step back, allowing you to ask: Is this the right way *for me*? Do my goals line up with what motivates me?

Motivation is the key to everything. Without motivation, eventually your dreams will dissipate into the sky. Knowing exactly what motivates you helps you find the career that's truly fulfilling—your true north.

My friend Jamie believed self-publishing was her path to success. She worked hard getting her first book professionally edited, designed, and released under her own publishing imprint. She was thrilled at first, but after a few months she became discouraged because no one was contacting her to talk about her book. Turns out she was motivated more by *connection* than she was by *independence* or *freedom*. When self-publishing didn't bring her fulfillment, she thought she'd either done something wrong or her writing wasn't good enough.

The real problem was that Jamie didn't understand what truly motivated her. If she had, she might have put more time and energy into creating a vibrant blog or posting on social media where she could attract more readers and interact with them. That by itself would have contributed to her fulfillment, and establishing a group of friends and fans first would have also increased her odds of making connections that would have helped her get the word out about her self-published book.

David had a different problem. He quickly wrote, self-edited, and self-published a book and then put a significant financial investment into marketing it. The book sold fairly well. It had an attractive cover and intriguing premise, enough that readers were induced to buy it. It didn't, however, do well in the contests he entered. He also received several three-star and lower ratings, which caused him to second-guess his writing talent. This self-doubt slowed him down on his next book project, shaking his confidence and making it more difficult for him to power through and finish it.

David, you see, was motivated by *achievement* and *recognition*. If he'd known that, he might have put more time into editing the book to increase its quality. That would have given him better odds of gaining the recognition and praise he desired in contests and reviews.

Whatever motivates you, embrace it. Maybe you're ashamed to admit what you really want to do is influence people. Maybe your friends or your siblings have told you to keep your advice to yourself, so you hesitate to follow your natural inclinations when it comes to your writing and platform activities. If this is your motivation, though, and you decide to use it to your advantage, you could be of great service to a lot of individuals. Look at all the other writers who do influence others and thoroughly enjoy it. Check out heavily quoted, influential blogs and books and if that excites you, that's the direction you need to go, no matter what little brother or sister says.

More than anything, Robert wanted to cut back on his work hours to spend more time on creative projects he chose for himself. Thinking he could make some extra money selling his own books, he—like Jamie—spent over a year writing, editing, and publishing his book, only to hear crickets once it came out. He despaired, thinking he would never find a way to get out of the rat race he was in. His plan to make money with self-publishing—which he thought would give him the freedom to cut back on his hours at work—hadn't panned out, and he was lost.

If Robert had fully understood that his motivation was *freedom* and *independence*, he would have looked more carefully into the publishing business and learned that his plan was unlikely to result in extra income, since it's extremely rare for a writer to earn substantial funds from one book. Perhaps a better plan would have been to try freelancing instead, writing blogs, reports, or website copy for clients—something that would have brought in real money in a short period of time. Had he been more self-aware, he would have saved himself over a year of work and struggle and more easily achieved his goal.

What motivates you? The more you can zero in on that, the more you can create and follow directions that will bring you closer to your goal, rather than going down some other road you shouldn't be following.

Using Your Intuition to Find Your True North

Another writing friend of mine, Jeri Walker, is an English teacher who always wanted to write fiction. She tried it for years, but kept running up against a wall of self-doubt and writer's block. Eventually she quit her job in the education system and started building her own freelance editing business. She was just getting that off the ground when she was diagnosed with breast cancer.

That diagnosis forced Jeri to stop and focus on her health. In the midst of all the chemotherapy, radiation, and surgical treatments, she turned to the one thing that had always brought her comfort: writing. Since she had to cut back on her work hours, she started a blog on a funding webpage in an effort to raise money to help pay the bills.

"In my darkest hours, words have always seen me through," she wrote on *Writing and Wellness*. "Writing leads to thoughts and thinking brings perspective." And later, "This writing is me doing the work of saving myself. Nothing more. Nothing less. If others read it, great."

As time passed, however, Jeri's writing began to move in a new direction. She found the blogs she was sharing about her cancer experience were not only helping her, they were helping her connect with others. "What I hadn't planned on was receiving so many private messages from people who've shared things about their own struggles." She wasn't experiencing writer's block anymore. She'd found her way home. "I'd struggled for years over what I should be writing about. I'd studied both fiction and narrative nonfiction in college and could never quite concede my writing path sided with the less glamorous side of writing about the truth rather than making stuff up."

Jeri found her voice by letting her heart and intuition lead her. After her funding campaign, she realized that voice wanted to write a memoir. At the time of this writing, she's working on that project by creating shorter pieces for publication, which she'll eventually combine into a complete manuscript.

Another friend of mine wrote fantasy novels for a while, but after hearing a successful novelist speak at a convention about "writing fast," she turned her attention to romance novels, as she knew she could write those more quickly. A few years and many books later, she told me she felt as if she had found her "home" as a writer. Though she planned to return to fantasy at some point, romance was where she felt she belonged.

Of course, this isn't just about genre. It's about everything you do to support your writing. Alexandria Constantinova Szeman, author of the *New York Times Book Review's* Notable Book *The Kommandant's Mistress,* found new ways to connect with others through social media when she opened up about the abuse she had suffered as a child.

"The biggest emotional challenge in my writing career," Szeman wrote on *Writing and Wellness,* "has always been dealing with my childhood sexual abuse and rapes (by my father, stepfather, and mother [with implements]), and with the Munchausen Syndrome by Proxy (MSBP) abuse inflicted by my mother." Alexandria had written about abuse in her novel, but she thought since it was fiction, she would be protected from the emotional pain. Instead, it caused all of her own pain to resurface.

"Though none of the rapes in the novel is graphic, writing them caused all my own physical, psychological, and emotional pain to resurface." Later, she turned to writing her own memoir, *M is for Munchers: The Serial Killers Next Door.* In that book, she talked more about the abuse she suffered from her own mother. "Writing the memoir caused me at least as much emotional pain as writing the rape and sexual abuse scenes for my first novel had, if only because I was not hiding behind the mask of fiction but openly writing about my own life and family."

Alexandria published the book but was still dealing with the trauma when she started sharing on social media. "Surprisingly, one of the most healing influences of the emotional trauma of writing—besides putting my own abuse into books and being in therapy for almost 20 years—has been social media, which I joined in 2010.... I've become more comfortable sharing my own story of severe abuse and have become a survivor rather than a victim. I've even written several blog posts about the abuse I suffered. Having an empathetic group of fellow survivors connecting with me on social media, as well as through my blog posts and books, has helped me feel less isolated."

This is another good example of a writer following her own path and her own voice to connect with readers. The more Alexandria shared her story, the more readers spoke up about their own experiences, motivating her to continue to reach out.

You, too, can find unique ways to use your strengths and your story to draw readers to you. The key is to step back and examine the path you're following, and ask yourself, "Who put me on this path?" Was it you or someone else? And either way, is it the path you should be on now?

Discover More: Goals

Think about what goals you've been chasing up until now. Then ask yourself:

> If I achieve this goal, will it fulfill my primary motivation (the one you discovered from the quiz at the beginning of the chapter)?

____ Yes ____ No

> From what I've learned so far, am I motivated by something different than I initially thought?

____ Yes ____ No

Based on your answers to the above two questions, brainstorm ideas for how you might use your writing in a way that matches your primary motivation. In addition to your books, what other creative writing projects might fit? List at least five below.

Remember, there are many options! Some examples include writing for print or online magazines, blogging, podcasting, video blogging, speaking, creating workshops, selling reports or booklets, freelance writing or editing, ghostwriting, grant writing for causes you care about, creating your own online magazine, interviewing others for inspiring stories to share, and writing stories for your church or club publication. Keep brainstorming until you find something that excites you, then hold onto that idea and continue reading!

1. _____
2. _____
3. _____
4. _____
5. _____

PART II
YOUR PERSONAL PORTRAIT

"I believe that every person is born with talent."

~MAYA ANGELOU

CHAPTER 5

FOCUS ON THE GOOD STUFF

I BEGAN MY WRITING journey writing children's stories. I pictured myself as a children's writer because I'd spent most of my life teaching. Even as a kindergartener myself, the teacher asked me to help mentor other kids, and it's something I've continued to do throughout my life.

My first published short story was a children's story, but the more I wrote, the more I realized my brain wanted to tackle more mature subjects. After a couple years, I moved to adult short stories, but that didn't quite fit either—I longed for more space to develop characters, so after a few more years, I started writing novels. My first attempts were pure fantasy, of the dragon and griffin kind. I had fun writing those stories and got my first traditional publishing contract with one of them, but along the way I gravitated toward a more literary form of writing. I didn't actually find my niche in fiction until many years later when I had drafted six different novels. My journey to finding a unique and buildable author platform took even longer.

Sometimes you just need to write and write to discover what type of writing works for you. There's definitely something to be said for the "one million words to competency" idea. Fantasy author David Eddings famously said, "My advice to the young writer is likely to be unpalatable in an age of instant successes and meteoric falls. I tell the neophyte: Write a million words—the absolute best you can write, then throw it all away and bravely turn your back on what you have written. At that point, you're ready to begin."

So yes, you need to write a lot to discover what type of writing best fits your unique creative nature, but there's much more to creating a writing career than that. You need to find readers, and the best way to do that is to focus on your strengths in writing, creativity, and personality. Initially, that may feel strange. After all, aren't writers supposed to succeed by finding what their weaknesses are and then work on fixing those?

Focusing on Weakness Is a Bad Idea

You create a story and take it somewhere for feedback, maybe to a writer's group, some writing friends, a contest that offers critiques, a workshop, or you hire an editor. Your ultimate goal is to get feedback, and that's a good goal. But when you get that feedback, what do you focus on?

If you're like most writers, you zero in on your weaknesses, or on what you feel you did wrong. Seemingly forgotten are all those comments describing what you did well. Sure, it felt good to read those, but within a few minutes you've moved on and are thinking about where your story needs work. In reality, this is how we improve. We fix problem areas and the story gets better and our chances of being published increase.

Except this rarely happens. Instead, you work for months, or maybe years, trying to fix what's wrong with this one story, and odds are what you'll have to show for it will be a slightly better story, but one that's still not good enough to attract the eye of an agent or editor.

What happened? Your writing coach or group or editor or whoever it was had said your dialogue was weak, and you needed to speed up the pacing. You worked on both and afterward "they" said it was better. So why didn't you get the result you were hoping for?

Making a weakness less of a weakness is not enough to make you competitive in today's market. Competition is too fierce. You have to create the best story you're capable of creating, and trying to do that by focusing mostly on your weak areas is not going to get you where you want to be.

This is the same in other professions. Imagine you're mechanically inclined and were born with the natural ability to use your hands, but you're lousy at paper work. You want to start your own business as a mechanic, so you spend hours trying to get better at paper work. Five years later you may have slightly improved at keeping records, but meanwhile your business never got off the ground because you were spending so much time on your weakness that you neglected your strength, which was your mechanical work.

Thinking you can reach your highest potential by focusing on your weaknesses is like thinking you can make a horse a house pet if only you work hard enough at it. Yes, it's possible, but it's a lot less likely than just getting a dog or cat instead. Stephen King writes horror novels for a reason. If he had tried to improve the romance in his stories, he may not have experienced the level of success he has. It's the same reason Lee Child writes thrillers, and why George R.

R. Martin writes fantasy. I'm not saying you have to be stuck in one genre, but it's undeniable that each writer tends to have a skill in a certain type of writing. You just have to find yours.

Bestselling author Paul B. Brown wrote in *Forbes*, "You are far better off capitalizing on what you do best, instead of trying to offset your weakness. Making a weakness less of a weakness is simply not as good as being the best you possibly can be at something."

I'm not saying you should ignore your weaknesses completely. When I first started writing novels, I hired an editor and got feedback that was really helpful. She pointed out my weaknesses, and I spent a good amount of time studying plot, story structure, conflict, and suspense. It was time well spent as we all need to educate ourselves in the craft of writing. The problem was that I spent *more* time on those things than I did building my strengths, which slowed my progress considerably.

Focus More on Your Strengths

Imagine you're in a classroom with three students and they're all about seven years old. Diana is attentive and bright, but she seems afraid to speak up. Skylar is a rowdy boy and frequently disruptive but is particularly good with numbers. Michael is adorable and sweet, but seems to be a little slow when it comes to learning.

It's up to you to help each child live up to his or her full potential. Playing to each child's strengths is the key. It's not going to help to approach Skylar with a heavy hand when trying to get him to sit still and be quiet. All that's going to do is create a fight that makes losers of you both. It's not going to help to call Diana out and try to get her to answer a question, as she'll only shrink more deeply into herself. And pushing Michael will likely ruin his sweet demeanor.

A better approach would be to ask Skylar, because of his energy and natural tendency to want to be the focus of attention, to lead one of the math lessons. Get him up out of his chair and have him lead a game that incorporates math practice. Allow Diana to create something at home she can bring to school to show the others, perhaps a model or art project or short story. Put Michael in charge of welcoming new students, and let him know that since he's so kind and gentle, he's the perfect one to help a new or lonely student feel more comfortable in class.

Taking these steps helps each student feel special, and by playing to their strengths, you help each one grow and improve. Skylar finds out that it's pretty fun playing teacher and looks forward to mentoring the other kids whenever you give him the opportunity, thereby being less disruptive. Diana gets some positive feedback for her projects, which helps her make friends and builds her confidence. Michael realizes that though he may not learn as quickly as the other kids, he's important to the class, which can help him build confidence that will likely show through the next time he tries to learn something.

When we focus on what we're good at, inevitably the process helps us improve our weaknesses as well. Writing coach Amy Benson Brown said as much when she wrote on the *Academic Coaching & Writing* blog, "I've found in coaching writers that … getting clarity on your strengths ultimately helps you improve weaker areas of your writing."

Unfortunately, we writers rarely think much about our strengths. We're far too busy focusing on our flaws. Indeed, psychologists have discovered that it's just human nature to pay attention to what's wrong most of the time.

Overcome Your Natural Tendency to Focus on the Negative

You've probably noticed the evening news is full of murders, disasters, and tragedies. There's a reason for that—humans, in general, put more weight on negative information. In a 2013 study on the topic, researchers Vaish and colleagues noted that we adults have a tendency, when faced with both positive and negative information, to focus "far more" on the negative, using it to guide our learning and decision-making.

Even from an early age, we're wired to pay more attention to bad news. Scientists have found that infants respond most powerfully to a mother's negative or fearful facial or vocal cues, compared to her positive or neutral ones. When exploring new toys, for instance, infants kept their distance from toys that were associated with a mother's look of disgust or verbal expression of fear, but if the mother expressed a happy response to a toy, the infant's response didn't differ much from when the mother expressed a neutral response.

Other experiments have shown similar results. By the age of three, most children are using about an equal number of positive and negative words, but after the age of three, the use of negative words almost doubles. When toddlers talked to their mothers, they were also found to focus mainly on negative events—such as when they were hurt—rather than on positive ones. Children five to twelve years old were also observed recalling negative events with more descriptive details than positive events.

Negativity is not intrinsic. Scientists don't think we're born with an inclination for it. Instead, it seems we learn the negativity bias early on. Infants younger than six months, for example, focused longer on pictures of happy faces than fearful, angry, or neutral ones, and responded more to happy voices than angry or sad ones. But between the ages of seven and twelve months, that behavior changed—infants were more likely to look longer at fearful rather than happy faces, and to respond more to angry and fearful voices.

Scientists aren't sure why this occurs, but they theorize that infants quickly learn what situations are threatening and become more vigilant to signs of danger. Another theory asserts that infants are normally presented with positive situations, so negative ones are perceived as unusual and demand more of their attention. Still another theory states that a mother's interaction with an infant tends to be mostly positive until the child starts crawling—between the ages of seven and eight months—at which point she begins to warn that child of danger, introducing negative experiences.

Whatever the reason, this negative bias continues as we age. Many think it serves an evolutionary purpose—if we're always on the lookout for danger, we're more likely to stay safe and reproduce. What matters is that you become aware that negativity is a part of who you are, and if you're not careful, it can hinder your progress as a writer.

Negative Bias Slows Progress

Considering the research, it may make more sense why one negative comment from a reader (or from anyone, for that matter) has the ability to loom so large in your mind. The human brain's negative bias means you're more sensitive to bad news. Research on adults using brain scans found that the brain had a greater surge in electrical activity when subjects were shown negative images than when they were shown positive ones. That means we give more emotional weight to negative news, such as a rejection or bad review. If you want to keep writing long-term, you need five positive comments (or more) to offset just one negative one.

Let's take a look at relationships. Scientists have discovered an ideal ratio of positive-to-negative interactions in couples that actually "make it." That magic ratio was the same five-to-one. As long as the couple experienced five positives for every one negative, the relationship was likely to remain stable. Those experiencing fewer positive experiences than that (and more negative ones) were more likely to break up during the study period.

Think of your relationship with your writing in the same way. That relationship is capable of creating a long and fulfilling career for you as long as you continue to experience five times as many positive experiences as negative ones. When that ratio becomes skewed, you're most likely to doubt yourself or potentially even quit writing altogether.

We tend to elevate negative information far beyond the importance it deserves, and that's destructive not only to a writing career, but to life in general. Knowing this, let's look at the advice most writers receive early on in their careers: attend a writers' group, go to a writers' workshop, and/or somehow submit your work for feedback. When you do this, you open yourself up to that one thing we all struggle with: criticism.

Much of the time, editorial critiques weigh heavily on the negative. Sure, a reader may indicate she liked one scene or related well to one character, but then she'll be sure to point out all the scenes that confused her, the dialogue that didn't seem to fit, the chapter where she got bored, and the setting details that seemed out of place. You, the writer, are likely to come out of such an experience reeling with self-doubt and discouragement, from which it often takes a long time to recover unless you know how to counter it.

This is a double-edged sword since you can't learn how to improve your writing if you don't open yourself up to feedback. To avoid becoming roadkill on the path to publishing success, you must learn how to overcome negative bias and focus on strengths more than weaknesses.

Actions for Overcoming Negative Bias

First, accept your own negative bias. The more you become aware of how you respond to feedback, the better you'll get at dealing with it. Without this self-awareness, you may simply focus on the negative and drown in your disappointment. That's the fastest way to failure as a writer and as a person.

When negative thoughts start creeping into your mind, or when you find yourself mulling over a reader or editor's negative comment, shake yourself awake. Tell yourself: "This is my brain focusing too much on the negative." Then take some action to disrupt your thought path. Call a good friend, review your accomplishments, read a positive comment from a reader, go take a walk, or listen to some happy music. The point is to get yourself out of "ruminating" mode so you are able to look at the situation more objectively and interrupt the brain's tendency to drag you down.

Next, find ways to actively combat the tendency to think negatively about yourself and your writing. One of the easiest ways is by keeping track of any and every positive comment you receive. Because we give less weight to this good feedback, we have to frequently remind ourselves about it. Keep positive comments from editors, workshop instructors and participants, agents, readers, and whoever else supplies them. Think of creative ways to display these comments so you have ready access to them—say, on your computer wallpaper, as printouts on a corkboard, or in a list you can easily pull up and read. Reviewing the positive stuff regularly helps you keep the negative gunk at bay and in perspective.

I'd recommend you spend at least a few minutes each month going over all the good comments you've received. Check back on the websites that listed your story as a finalist in a contest, or those containing posts you wrote that received favorable feedback. If an editor or agent praised your writing in an email, print out that email and keep it in a file of only positive comments. Review this file as often as you need to. Take ten to fifteen minutes re-reading these, as research has shown you need at least that long for the information to really sink into your mind. Otherwise it will quickly disappear like it did the first time.

According to neuropsychologist Rick Hanson, PhD and author of *Buddha's Brain: The Practical Neuroscience of Happiness, Love, and Wisdom*, "the brain is like Velcro for negative experiences and Teflon for positive ones." This can make it difficult for you to build your confidence as a writer. The next time you receive positive feedback, take the time to enjoy it, savor it, and allow it to lift you up. Go celebrate with a dinner out or some unexpected free time. When you allow a positive experience to shape you, you're not being self-indulgent, you're being smart about encouraging your inner artist.

The Next Step: Find and Focus on Your Strengths

Who are you as a writer? That's a deceptively simple question and the answer may take you years to truly discover. That's okay, as long as you start focusing on your strengths right now. To begin, you first have to know where you're going, and you can't know that until you better understand your talents, skills, passions, and motivations. I'm going to help you delve into this more as we go along, but for now, start making note of those things that are working in your writing life.

If you find, for example, people respond to your blog posts about travel, you can build on that by writing more. If your last critique pointed out that your story was exciting and fast-moving, focus on that for a bit. Find out where that was working and how you can use that skill again in another fast-moving scene. If you excelled in your debate team in high school or college, consider working that skill into your writing platform. Maybe you could do public speaking events, conduct workshops, speak in the schools or libraries, or even create instructional videos.

You don't have to make any big decisions now, just start keeping your eye out for these things. The more you recognize and take note of them, the more motivation you'll have with your writing and your platform.

To prove this to yourself, think back to the things you did as a child. Maybe your parents insisted on piano lessons, but you hated them. Put a baseball bat in your hand, though, and you could practice hitting all day long. At which activity did you end up excelling? Most likely it was baseball. Given the chance, we're more motivated to practice and work hard at those things for which we have a natural inclination.

The same thing happens as an adult. Let's say you take a job at a call center, but you're extremely introverted and talking to people on the phone all day drains your energy and puts you in a bad mood. Then you get a chance to work for a company as a graphic designer. You get to sit at your computer alone and produce good-looking ads that clients love. In which job do you think you'll be more likely to receive a promotion?

The Benefits of Focusing on Your Strengths

Focusing on your strengths doesn't mean you'll ignore your weaknesses. Instead, it's a strategy for discovering that unique niche that will draw readers to your platform.

When you focus on your strengths, the following happens:

- You'll build confidence more easily.

- You'll feel more energized and motivated.

- You'll have more positive emotions about what you're doing.

- You'll feel less stress and anxiety, and happier in general.

- You'll experience faster growth as a writer.

- You'll be more likely to find what's unique about you that you can then use to increase your visibility.

- You'll be more satisfied with your writing career.

Convinced? Great. Let's get busy finding out what *you're* particularly good at.

Discover More: List Your Strengths

Using your journal, record your answers to the following questions. It's okay if you're not sure at this point. This is just to get you started thinking, so make your best guess for the time being. Then keep this page handy as we'll add to it again later.

1. **List three strengths you have as a writer.** Examples include: realistic dialogue, great setting descriptions, well-drawn characters, rich prose, "clean writing" (good spelling, grammar), and ability to create vivid mental pictures.

2. **List three strengths you have as a storyteller/content writer.** Examples include: ability to write a fast-moving plot, create likeable characters, thrill or scare the reader, comfort the reader, cause the reader to think, evoke strong emotions, inform the reader, and make complex subjects easy to understand.

3. **List three strengths you have as a person that might apply to your writing career.** Examples include: you're entertaining, funny, caring, personable, creative, crafty, organized, adventurous, smart, helpful, artistic, or musical.

CHAPTER 6

IDENTIFY YOUR STRENGTHS

D
ON'T THINK THE only strengths that matter when it comes to your writing world are those directly related to writing. The truth is, to expand your reach and gain a reader's attention, you need to bring all your strengths to your writing platform.

"Realizing our strengths is the smallest thing we can do to make the most difference," said Alex Linley, PhD, psychologist and co-author of *The Strengths Book: Be Confident, Be Successful, and Enjoy Better Relationships by Realising the Best of You.*

How can you make a difference in your reader's world? That's the question you want to ask yourself. You may usually wonder, *How can I get the reader to buy my book?* Instead, ask, "How can I intrigue the reader so she'll *want* to buy my book?"

How indeed? Start by figuring out exactly what your strengths are as an individual. An interesting study by Gallup of nearly 50,000 business workgroups in forty-five countries found those who helped capitalize on the strengths of their employees experienced more success than those who didn't. Those who ran strengths-based work-shops saw increases in sales and profits. They also helped reduce turnover and improve employee engagement.

Five Ways Knowledge of Your Strengths Benefits Your Writing Career

When you identify and purposely capitalize on your strengths, you'll begin to notice certain benefits in your writing career.

1. You'll feel more energized and motivated.

Think about how you feel when you're doing something you're good at. Maybe that's skiing, or writing, or fixing the car, or build-ing something. Whatever it is, when you're doing it, you're enjoying yourself. You have energy, and you don't mind doing that activity for an extended period.

On the other hand, when you do something you're not so good at, time tends to drag, and you're likely to feel fatigued more quickly. You'll watch the clock and wait for that moment when you can finally escape.

Whenever you tap into your strengths, you tap into your energy. As a freelance writer, for example, I frequently get assignments that initially sound boring. I may have to write about a certain herb that I could care less about or write for the umpteenth time about foods that help relieve pain. That's when I tap into my natural strength of "curiosity" to find something about the topic that piques my interest. This technique works most all the time, as inevitably I'll find some bit of information that intrigues me, and then I'm off and running.

When you learn what your strengths are, you can apply this strat-egy to your writing world. Let's say marketing your books makes you feel uncomfortable. What if you could find some way to enjoy it? Maybe you like getting people together for fun activities. You're a natural host or hostess! You could apply this talent to your book launches, book signings, and more. Then marketing would be a fun activity, and you'd feel energized and motivated when doing it.

2. You'll boost your confidence.

Thinking too much about what you may be doing wrong leads to negative emotions that can kill your self-esteem. Psychologist Paula Durlofsky, PhD, wrote in her blog, *Uploading Hope*, "Focusing on weaknesses while ignoring strengths creates feelings of discouragement, failure, low self-esteem, and can even contribute to depression."

As a writer and creator, you must be sure you're building your strengths *more* than addressing your weaknesses. When you're participating in an activity you have a natural talent for, you'll feel more confident doing it, even if you haven't fully developed that skill yet.

If you have a good sense of humor and you can make others laugh, you likely get a boost of confidence whenever you use that strength. Fine-tune it, practice it, use it more often in your blogs, videos, social media posts, and even in your workshops and book readings down the road. Tapping into that strength will make most all of your activities easier and more rewarding.

3. You'll experience less stress and more well-being.

"In my research with Reena Govindji," psychologist Alex Linley said, "we have shown that using our strengths is associated with higher levels of subjective well-being and psychological well-being, even when controlling for self-esteem and self-efficacy."

We writers often live stressful lives. We get overwhelmed with all that's involved in supporting our books and other projects. The solution is to focus on your strengths. It helps relieve stress and may even make you a happier person. Having consistent experiences that maintain good feelings improves your mood, increasing your ability to handle setbacks. If you're regularly incorporating activities in your day that you're good at, you'll wake up more energized and more motivated to go after your goals.

4. You'll stop worrying about being good at everything.

Many people feel pressured today to be good at everything. They imagine they must be the perfect employees, friends, spouses, parents, and community members, while penning bestsellers, knitting fashionable sweaters, whisking homemade meals off to the elderly, and running the occasional marathon. Adopting a "build your strengths" mindset can help a person let go of that high-stress attitude. Everyone has certain things they're good at, and certain things they're not so good at, and that's okay (and why we need each other!).

In their book *Strengths-based Leadership*, authors Tom Rath and Barrie Conchie wrote, "If you spend your life trying to be good at everything, you will never be great at anything. While our society encourages us to be well-rounded, this approach inadvertently breeds mediocrity." So go a little easier on yourself. You don't have to be super-mom, super-woman, super-employee, super-baker, super-writer, and super-interior decorator. Keep focusing on what you do well, and as for the rest, do the best you can do, and then let it go.

5. You'll be more likely to inspire others.

Think about a person who inspires you and then ask yourself why that is. Most likely, it has something to do with what she's good at.

Your mom is naturally caring and compassionate, your uncle can create amazing things with wood, your brother always knows how to fix your car, or so-and-so writer has a way of sucking you into her story within a single paragraph. It's usually not because people are "nice" or "polite" that you admire them—it's because of their unique talents and gifts.

When you focus on building your strengths, you give yourself a chance to soar to your highest possible level, becoming the best possible version of yourself.

How Talent Morphs into Strength

A good place to start identifying our strengths is to look back on our childhood and adolescent years when our unique talents first begin to surface. When we are young, we act with no pretense. We haven't yet started to hide certain parts of ourselves or to label them "good" or "bad." By going back in your memory you can more easily figure out what your basic, raw gifts were. Often these are the gifts that eventually morphed into strengths as you aged.

My early talent for teaching and mentoring, for example, morphed into my current strength as a teacher and workshop leader. My commitment to always turn in my homework on time morphed into the strength of "discipline," which has served me well as a self-employed professional. My desire to escape to some sort of dream world—using a book, a horseback ride, or my own imagination—morphed into a strength in my current creative work.

Look back on your life and think about some of the earliest indications of your gifts and talents to find what your strengths are (or could be) today. The questions and prompts below may help stimulate your memory. Record your answers in your journal or notebook.

Early Talents that Indicate Possible Strengths

1. What did you love to do even as a young child? Name just one—the first one that comes to mind.

2. What was your favorite subject in school? (If you didn't enjoy school, name one activity you dreamed about doing instead.)

3. What is the earliest memory of a person telling you that you did something well, and what was it you did?

4. What was your favorite pastime when you weren't in school, doing homework, or engaged in some other organized activity? In other words, when your time was all your own, what did you do with it?

5. Name two or three activities at which you excelled as you got older. These could include sports activities, classes in school, or after-school activities.

6. What was it about you that your friends liked or commented on? What did they say stood out about you? Were you funny, smart, a good listener, supportive, a leader, athletic, popular?

7. When you were young, what did you dream about doing when you grew up? Why do you think that appealed to you?

8. If you could name one thing that got you through your childhood, what would it be? (Examples might include your imagination, humor, confidence, inner strength, courage, big heart, brains, and ability to make friends.)

9. Name two of your childhood heroes and why you admired them.

10. Think back to those silly high school yearbook "best at" or "most likely to" lists. Maybe you were selected for one of them, maybe you weren't, but if you had been able to choose one for yourself, which one would it have been? (Examples might include smartest, funniest, biggest flirt, most creative, most likely to be president, most adventurous, or feel free to make one up!)

Dig a Little Deeper

Now I'd like you to look over each of your answers and then list what strength you were displaying at the time. If your answer to number one was "read," for example, it could be that you easily understood language from an early age, but it could also be that you were naturally imaginative or curious, liked to be challenged so you could think more deeply, or enjoyed putting clues together to figure out a mystery.

Take your answer, whatever it was, and change it into a strength. If your answer to the first question was that you loved to play with dolls, your strength might be that you were caring and nurturing, or that you were intrigued by relationships. If your favorite subject in school was math, your strength may have been that you were analytical or that you were naturally good with numbers. If others told you were a fast runner, your strength may have been that you were athletic or driven. If your favorite thing to do on your own time was to draw or create mud pies, your strength may have been that you were creative or artistic.

Get the idea? Okay, give it a try. It doesn't have to be perfect, just do your best. Again, in your journal, change each of the answers you gave above to a strength.

1. What did you love to do even as a young child? (Think about your answer, and write down what strength or talent this activity was tapping into.)

Your Strength #1:

_____

2. What subject was your favorite in school? (Or out of school.)

Your Strength #2:

_____

3. What is the earliest thing you remember others telling you that you did well?

Your Strength #3:

_____

4. What was your favorite thing to do when your time was all your own?

Your Strength #4:

_____

5. Look at the two or three activities you excelled in and write down the strengths they indicated:

Your Strength #5:

_____

Your Strength #6:

_____

Your Strength #7:

_____

6. What was it about you that your friends liked or commented on?

Your Strength #8:

_____

7. When you were young, what did you dream about doing when you grew up?

Your Strength #9:

_____

8. What one personality trait got you through your childhood?

Your Strength #10:

_____

9. Look at your two childhood heroes and think about the characteristics you admired about them. Most likely, these characteristics are strengths of yours as well. Name one characteristic from each below.

Your Strength #11:

_____

Your Strength #12:

_____

10. Think about who you were in the high school yearbook "best at" or "most likely to" list. What strength did that imply? (If you were popular, maybe your strength was leadership or influence. If you were the funniest, maybe your strength was humor or ability to entertain. The most creative? Maybe your strength was a strong imagination, thinking outside the box, or a skilled painter.)

Your Strength #13:

_____

Keep your answers handy as you may refer to them again in later chapters. In fact, it's best if you keep a notebook or file specifically devoted to your strengths, as referring back to them will continue to serve you throughout your life.

You Can Use Any Strength or Skill to Help Propel Your Writing Career

You might wonder what these early strengths have to do with your writing career now. In some cases, the connection is clear—if you were a creative young person, obviously it fits that you'd be a writer now. In other cases, it may not be so clear. If you were a math whiz, but now you're a writer, it can be difficult to see the connection. The point is to broaden your thinking about what you do well and how you can apply those early skills to your creative career.

Let's say you were popular in school. You may think that has nothing to do with your writing, but hold on a minute. That early experience may have indicated that one of your strengths was as an influencer, or maybe you were a natural leader. You could use the same strength in your social media posts or in your blogs to help build your audience. You could capitalize on it even further if you decided to start a new club or group, a new nonprofit organization, a new writing retreat, or if you wanted to write a nonfiction book on a subject you're passionate about.

The only thing limiting you is your imagination. Once you start to discover your strengths, all you need to do is find new ways to use them to attract more readers. Linda L. Osmundson, for example, a children's author who appeared on *Writing and Wellness*, had nearly given up on her dream of publishing a book when she just happened to become a docent for several local museums.

"I served as a docent in four art museums and two galleries," Linda wrote, "gave hundreds of tours, and taught docents and classroom volunteers how to induce children to interact with art. Those experiences soon turned into my 'looking at art' picture books."

Linda combined her skills as a docent with her love of children's literature to create three different children's books: "To create my first art picture book, I chose a favorite western artist: Charles Russell. I narrowed it down to thirteen of his images and adapted the format from my tours for *How the West Was Drawn: Charles Russell's Art*. Questions encouraged readers to look at his pictures and then read 250 words about the artist and/or the image. Pelican Publishing purchased the manuscript and my first book was released in 2011."

That decision to tap into the strengths she had outside of writing marked the beginning of Linda's writing career: "When I received the five boxes I'd ordered after the release, I was 72. I opened a box, withdrew a copy, saw my name on the cover, and cried."

Linda's story is inspiring as it shows how you're never too old to take a new skill, interest, or strength and turn it into a way to make your writing dreams come true.

Choose Your Strengths

Here's another strength exercise for you. I've listed a number of personality traits below. All of these strengths could be used to increase your odds of experiencing creative career success. Look the list over and choose the five traits you think most apply to you.

Ready? Here's the list:

Action-oriented	Disciplined	Adventurous	Organized
Artistic	Focused	Communicative	Responsible
Compassionate/ Caring	Intelligent	Curious	Good People Skills
Courageous	Patient	Fast Learner	Intuitive
Confident	Determined	Emotionally Intelligent	Inspiring
Outgoing	Visionary	Funny	Entertaining
Detail Oriented	Creative	Charming	Optimistic
Flexible	Persistent	Helpful	Natural Leader
Analytical	Problem Solver	Good Listener	Teacher
Thoughtful	Thinker	Empathetic	Generous
Honest	Independent	Observant	Persuasive
Spiritual	Warm	Wise	Encouraging

In your journal, write down the five traits you chose, in any order:

- _____

- _____

- _____

- _____

- _____

Now examine these five traits again and organize them in order of strongest to weakest.

1. _____

2. _____

3. _____

4. _____

5. _____

Finally, look back over the list again. Is there a trait you think truly describes you that wasn't on the list? If so, write that trait down, then insert it where you think it belongs in the list of five above. If not, go ahead to the next section.

Extra trait: _____

New list of six traits (optional):

1. _____

2. _____

3. _____

4. _____

5. _____

6. _____

Feeling Stronger?

Transfer each of the strengths you found in this chapter to a master "strengths" document. We're going to keep adding to that document, so by the time you finish this book, you'll have a powerful reference tool to use when looking for new ways to boost your career. (It's also helpful when you're going through periods of self-doubt!)

Discover More: Find More of Your Strengths

Let's dig into your strengths a little bit more. Answer the following questions, and add these answers to the others you created for this chapter. See if you find any that are repeating—strengths popping up in more than one exercise. Pay special attention to these as they are likely some of your strongest traits.

1. Name one activity that when it's over, you immediately want to do it again. Name the strength you're tapping into while doing this activity:

2. What one activity do you procrastinate on again and again? Name the weakness that makes this activity difficult:

3. What was the last achievement you felt super-proud of? Name the main strength you used to obtain this achievement:

4. Name one activity where you bring a unique approach—the activity that causes your friends or family to say, "Oh, I never thought of doing it that way!" Name the strength you were displaying during that activity:

Now list the three strengths and one weakness you discovered and keep track of these in your main notebook or document.

CHAPTER 7

DISCOVER YOUR HEROES

Who are your writing heroes? Can you name them right now?

I ask these questions a lot and what amazes me is how many blank looks I receive in response. Maybe it's because my own writing heroes are so important to the progress I've made as a writer. I can't fathom a serious writer not having writer heroes.

I'll even go so far as to say that if you're struggling as a writer, the solution may be to discover who your heroes are and actively pursue ways to see them in person, or listen to them speak on YouTube or in podcasts. At a minimum, you should be reading their work.

Here's why.

Who Inspired You to Write?

Writers may think they don't need writing heroes. We work in isolation. We explore the depths of our own imaginations to create. We research to discover what we don't know.

We are tasked with coming up with something original, so why would we be concerned about what other writers are doing? Couldn't that even be a little dangerous? After all, we don't want our own vision to be muddied or distracted by someone else's. And as I've mentioned, each writer has to forge his or her own path. So isn't it best just to focus on our own creativity?

To answer that question, I need to ask you another one: Who inspired you to be a writer? For most, the answer is: another writer. Somewhere along the way, someone's prose got your attention. You read something that stayed with you. Maybe you didn't instantly think, *Man, that was really cool. I want to do that too.* But you were changed, somehow, and you remembered that change.

I have had many of these experiences in my life. Books expanded my thinking, helped me imagine other places and other experiences, and gave me ideas for other ways I might approach life. I remember at the age of about twelve writing down every word of Edgar Allan Poe's "The Raven," just to feel the words flowing through my fingers and to relive their effects in my inner ear.

I bought Walter Farley's *Black Stallion* books because I loved horses, but it was his way of taking me into other worlds and other settings that stays with me to this day. Yet I never planned to be a writer. I never even thought about it until well after I'd completed my bachelor's degree in music. But I can look back now and know it was those other writers who gradually led me to this mode of expression, even if with invisible hands.

Adults Need Heroes Too

Kids are easily drawn to heroes, but as adults, it can be more difficult to find them because we're more likely to see the flaws in people. No longer are heroes as shiny and perfect as they were when we were children, and many fall from grace, so to speak, as we learn disappointing things about them.

"As we get older, we realize all people are flawed," wrote Scott T. Allison, psychologist and author of *Heroes: What They Do and Why We Need Them*. "As we get older, we recognize that even Gandhi had flaws and Martin Luther King Jr. had affairs and Mickey Mantle was a drunk and a womanizer."

But you need heroes even more as an adult than you did as a youngster—especially when you're a writer. They serve as real examples of the success you seek, and though you may not be able to follow the same path they did, you can still allow them to inspire you. From their stories of struggle you can learn how to overcome your own. As they describe their writing processes, their words can help validate your unique way of writing.

Where else are you going to discover this information? How else are you to learn how to manage the difficult journey that is writing?

Seven Reasons Heroes are Critical to the Writer's Journey

1. Heroes remind us of where we want to go.

It's easy for a writer to begin to settle for what he or she has, or has not, achieved. The writing path is a challenging one, and you'll encounter many difficulties along the way. You may get tired, discouraged, and depressed. You may begin to think you'll never do any better than you're doing at this moment.

I had an experience like this before my first book was published. In the final stages, I was facing some disappointments. The cover looked amateurish, but I couldn't change it. The marketing assistance I'd hoped for wasn't coming. What was supposed to be the shining moment I'd waited for (having a book traditionally published) was losing some of its sparkle. Despite my best efforts, I felt myself sliding into a low place, emotionally, just when I was supposed to be most high.

As luck (or providence) would have it, I happened to be in the right place at the right time to see one of my writing heroes, Andre Dubus III (*House of Sand and Fog*, among others) speak. His words about the writing journey, a writer's struggles, and a writer's purpose jolted me out of my doldrums and set me back on the path where I needed to be. He reminded me of the star I was chasing, and that the chase was worth it, no matter what.

Writing heroes show us what's possible, and what's *real*. When we listen to them, we're reminded that the way is difficult for everyone, even those who make success look easy. We realize the journey is supposed to be a struggle, and we're inspired to get back at it.

2. Heroes help us overcome difficulty.

When you're facing a difficulty in your writing, you can turn to writing mentors or other books, but in my experience, the real breakthroughs come from talking face-to-face with your heroes.

That happened to me once with Daniel Woodrell (*Winter's Bone*, among others). I attended a workshop that left me feeling confused and lost. Daniel was one of the guest writers at the event who gave a reading and interview, and I was lucky enough to find him alone on the sidewalk that night. I usually hate bothering people, particularly for my own personal issues (which can seem so small when standing next to someone so accomplished), but I was desperate, so I asked him how he would manage a problem like mine.

The advice he gave me was good, but what was even better was the way he gave it. He spoke to me like a fellow writer, one worthy of a thoughtful answer. In five minutes he lifted me up from where I'd fallen, which was thinking I'd deluded myself by believing I could write, and placed me back on my feet where I felt more confident about tackling the issue.

I've had other experiences like this—too many to relay here. There's just nothing like getting valuable advice directly from someone who's achieved the goals you're trying to achieve. It's not so that you can do the exact same thing they did, but so you can understand deep within yourself that the struggle is worth it.

3. Heroes give us clues about who we should become.

There's this thing I do before attending a conference or workshop. It was actually my mom's idea. She loves to travel and has attended many of these events with me. Since most writing events offer author readings or presentations that are free to the public, she suggested we scour the names of all the presenters, get copies of their books, and read as many as possible before going, so we would be more knowledgeable about the authors we'd be listening to.

What a great idea! I can't recommend it enough. We've done it several times now, and not only have I introduced myself to a number of outstanding writers this way, I've found more heroes who have been incredibly helpful in my career.

Another benefit of this practice is you discover more about the writer you want to be. Typically, as I'm reading in preparation for the event, one of the writers will stand out to me above the others. Often, that writer, when talking about her personal writing process, will share thoughts that could have come out of my own head and heart.

The qualities you admire in others, even if you don't realize it, are usually qualities you also possess. If you've ever heard one of your writing heroes describe his writing process and it mirrored your own process, you know the feeling—it's magical. Not only do you feel validated—your process is similar to that of this successful writer, so it can't be all crazy—but you may also feel a sense of peace, a reconnection with yourself.

Yes, you're on the right path. Just keep going.

4. Heroes help calm our self-doubt.

Writers often struggle with self-doubt. All you have to do is peruse the author interviews on *Writing and Wellness* and you'll see the issue come up again and again.

Sometimes, hearing one of our heroes speak inadvertently magnifies our self-doubt. Most successful writers are brilliant—really. It's common to be blown away by how smart, charismatic, deep, thoughtful, and generally amazing they are. *I could never be like that*, you're likely to think.

I've thought that sometimes in the presence of these masters, but the thought always vanishes once I start talking to them. On the whole, successful writers are helpful and encouraging people. They know what it's like to struggle. They've done it—and, if you listen closely, most continue to do so. They know they don't have all the answers, but they're willing to help however they can.

I had the distinct pleasure of meeting Hannah Tinti (*Animal Crackers* and other award-winning books). I asked her about book marketing and the struggle to balance new demands placed on authors, and she spent a good ten minutes encouraging me and giving me some great advice. She didn't have to—I'm sure she was tired after a long day of teaching and speaking—but I was extremely grateful she did.

Most of your writing heroes will encourage you. Those who don't, don't deserve to be your heroes. If you get a chance to talk to them, you'll see. There's nothing like encouragement from someone you really admire.

5. Heroes teach us how to respond in all sorts of situations.

Writers are expected to wear many hats these days. In addition to being writers and storytellers, we're now required to be marketers, business owners, bloggers, and more. Our heroes can serve as great examples of how to tackle these various roles.

I've watched Andre Dubus III do book signings several times, and when compared to other writers, he's a master. Instead of focusing on himself and his work, he turns the focus entirely on the person for whom he's signing the book. He seems genuinely interested in who she is, asking questions that encourage her to share. He gets up on his feet (instead of staying glued to his chair as many writers do), shakes hands, and makes the other person feel welcome and at ease. By the time he's finished signing the book, the reader feels as if she's made a new friend.

This is the way to secure a fan for life. I've worked to emulate this style whenever I sign my books and have enjoyed the warm exchanges it creates.

Writing heroes give you a glimpse into a variety of ways to market, create an author platform, present yourself on panels, conduct workshops, and more, introducing you to techniques you may decide to use as you build your own unique niche in the writing world.

6. Heroes lift us up.

When we encounter our writing heroes, they often have a way of lifting us up. They elevate us.

Research has born this out. Psychologist Jonathan Haidt, who has studied the way acts of compassion can inspire feelings of elevation in humans, wrote in the *Greater Good* online magazine: "Powerful moments of elevation, whether experienced first or second hand, sometimes seem to push a mental 'reset' button, wiping out feelings of cynicism and replacing them with feelings of hope, love, optimism, and a sense of moral inspiration."

Interesting note: Haidt was said to have borrowed the term "elevation" in this instance from Thomas Jefferson, who used the phrase moral elevation "to describe the euphoric feeling one gets when reading great literature," according to Scott Allison.

As writers, aren't we always trying to do better, to achieve more? Poet Robert Browning wrote that a "man's reach should exceed his grasp." Heroes are what we reach for.

7. Heroes show us how to be heroes ourselves.

If you admire a certain writer, and you understand that having this admiration means there's something inside you that is like him or her, then you owe it to yourself and the world to learn more about that person. That will naturally get you closer to fulfilling your own purpose—and to becoming the hero of your own life.

After spending time around my heroes in the writing world, I feel a deeper sense of purpose. My writing becomes more than just penning the stories in my head. I remember that I'm giving back as best I can to the world. It's not that I think one little story is going to make any big difference in global events. Being around my heroes, though, does make me think that what I'm doing is worthwhile, and worthy of every effort I can pour into it.

That's a good thing, because the writing journey is long and difficult and it's easy to get discouraged and begin to think it's all silly and self-indulgent. But if you're truly called to do it, you can't give up. You owe it to yourself to actively seek out your heroes and let them inspire you. Heroes encourage you to keep improving and to eventually become a hero yourself.

Who Are Your Heroes?

In the exercise below, I encourage you to write down your top five heroes. If you don't know who they are, it's time to do some more digging, find out who you admire and who you feel a certain kinship with. It's helpful if at least some of the ones on your list are writers, but they don't all have to live in the publishing world. You may have heroes in other areas of your life that inspire you—feel free to list those, as well.

If you don't know who your writing heroes are, start by listing some of your favorite novels and do a little research about the authors. It helps if you use contemporary novels written by authors who are still alive, as then you'll have a chance to listen to and perhaps see them in person.

Discover More: The People You Admire

Write down the top five people you admire most. (It's best if you include at least one or two writers on the list.) Next to each name, state two qualities that you admire about the person.

My Hero:

1. _____

What I Admire about Him/Her:

a) _____
b) _____

(Continue until you have five names down.)

Now look back on all the qualities you wrote down. Most likely, at least some of them are reflections of qualities you have yourself, even if yours are not fully developed yet. In your journal, write down the qualities you share with your heroes. If you're not sure, ask your family and friends for help. Show them the list of qualities and ask them which they think you have too.

CHAPTER 8

YOUR TOP TWO WAYS OF THINKING

O NCE YOU IDENTIFY your strengths, you may think the hard work is over, but in truth, it's just beginning. Even though a strength is something you're naturally good at, that doesn't mean it can't be improved upon. In fact, it's your strengths that offer the best avenue for personal and professional growth.

That may seem a little backward. Logic tells us that if you're good at something, you should be able to coast in that area and focus only on weak areas. Sure, that's possible, but it won't take you as far as building on your strengths will.

This chapter will help you identify two more strengths you have, based on the work of psychiatrist Carl Jung. You'll also learn how to use those strengths to boost your writing platform.

Discover How You Perceive and Make Judgments in the World

You've probably heard of the Myers-Briggs Type Indicator® (MBTI®). If you haven't, you can go online and take the test. This step isn't required to move forward in this chapter, but it might help in your understanding.

The Myers-Briggs test is based on the theory of psychological types created by psychiatrist Carl Jung, who believed people see the world, take in information, and make decisions differently. He then categorized these differences. Using this theory along with their own research data on personality types, Katherine Cook Briggs and her daughter Isabel Briggs Myers developed the MBTI questionnaire to help people determine what jobs may best suit them and how to better navigate their relationships.

In this chapter, we're going to focus more deeply on Jung's eight categories of thinking, what he refers to as "cognitive processes." Most people tend to be particularly good with two of them, while weak in another two. The other four exist more in the unconscious mind, and therefore are not as accessible to conscious control. They are often called shadow functions, and are likely to appear when you're stressed out or not at your best.

We can learn a lot about ourselves from the eight cognitive processes, but for the sake of simplicity, we're going to focus on just two: your primary and secondary ones, which we'll call your primary and secondary cognitive functions. Though you can discover these by taking the Myers-Briggs test, an easier and sometimes more accurate way is to read through the eight functions and see which ones you relate to the most.

Your Top Two Cognitive Functions

- **Your strongest function, also called your "primary function" or "hero function," is your dominant function.** It's fully developed at a young age, usually by the time you enter your teens. It is mostly unconscious—you do it without much effort. Because of that, you may not be aware that this is a strength you possess. It is such a huge part of you that you assume everyone else has it, too, when in reality, this is where you shine.

- **Your second strongest function, also called your "secondary function" or "support function," supports your dominant function.** It takes a bit longer to develop, and usually comes into full effect by the time you're twenty-one years old. This is one you're conscious of, and you can choose to use it or not, though you often do because it's a strength.

These two functions together account for how you operate most of the time. They're the two strengths you can rely on to serve you well in both your daily activities and in your writing/creative career.

If you take a Myers-Briggs test online and discover your four-letter code, you can determine your top two cognitive functions, but you can also determine them by looking at the following two categories. Choose which of the four options in each sounds most like you.

Category 1: Perceiving—How You Learn

1. **"Doing" or "Sensation" (Se):** You act on concrete data from the here and now. You are a keen observer of your environ-

ment and easily recognize "what is." You are good at adapting to new situations and others consider you a "doer"—someone who takes action. You love directly interacting with the outside world and are attuned to the present moment. You also like developing and maintaining aesthetically pleasing surroundings. <u>You learn best when you are interested in a topic and have the freedom to pursue it. You hate to feel confined.</u> Spontaneous, adaptable, adventurous.

2. **"Preserving" or "Memory" (Si):** You compare present facts and experiences to past experiences. You are detail oriented, organized, and structured. You like knowing what to expect. You believe in upholding traditions and preserving the past, and you often compare and contrast the past to the present, noticing changing patterns. You trust the "tried and true" and prefer to stick with what works rather than try something new just because it's new. You hold tight to your cherished memories. <u>You learn best when you feel safe, and feel uncomfortable in strange and confusing situations you weren't prepared for.</u> Reliable, trustworthy, nostalgic.

3. **"Exploration" or "Brainstorming" (Ne):** You like brainstorming ideas and often come up with many of them. You experiment to see how things will turn out and frequently notice possibilities others miss because you're always searching for underlying meanings and connections. You enjoy reading and broadening your understanding and may speak in technical terms others have difficulty following. As you explore, you make new connections between people, places,

and things. <u>You learn best when given novelty and freedom, and you dislike strict routines.</u> Detached, focused, technical.

4. **"Knowing" or "Perspectives" (Ni):** You receive insights and ideas that seem to come from nowhere—your "aha moments." You reflect on your experiences and have an intense, probing focus that leads to your insights. You can detect the hidden motivations of others and foresee what may happen in the future. You have a sense of internal knowing and rely on your hunches. You like enthusiastically and creatively expressing your perspectives and possibilities to others. <u>You learn best when given absolute quiet and distractions frustrate you.</u> Entrepreneurial, independent, inspiring.

Choose which of the above sounds most like you, and use the two-letter code to identify your type.

My category 1 strength is: _____

Category 2: Judging—How You Make Decisions

1. **"Effectiveness" or "Systemizing" (Te):** You are organized, structured, and orderly as well as frank and decisive. You value productivity and enjoy implementing systems and procedures to keep things running smoothly. You are all about efficiency and have a plan for every scenario. You may be involved in creating guidelines and rules, and you believe in giving people usable plans for getting things done. <u>You make decisions after consulting with credible sources that make</u>

logical sense and dislike inefficiency. Your question: "What works?" Efficient, logical, decisive.

2. **"Harmony" or "Persuading" (Fe):** You are concerned with the energy, moods, needs, and feelings of others. Extremely empathetic, you're good at bringing out other's gifts and strengths and helping them get to the root of their problems. You're happiest when those around you are happy too. You're more likely to speak up for others than for yourself and can be a crusader if you feel the need is there. You make decisions based on what's best for everyone, and you dislike conflict. Your question: "How can I get everyone's needs met?" Caring, nurturing, protective.

3. **"Contemplating" or "Accuracy" (Ti):** You make sense of the world by digging in to your own thoughts, contemplating and questioning. You develop models and systems to figure out how things work but may not bother explaining it to others. You stay impersonal to ensure fair and right decisions. Challenging problems or technical puzzles energize you, as you are a skilled troubleshooter. You make decisions based on what sounds logical and dislike contradictory beliefs or values. Your question: "What makes sense to me?" Accurate, precise, logical.

4. **"Authenticity" or "Empathizing" (Fi):** You're concerned with individuality, authenticity, and personal meaning. You have a strong internal system of right and wrong and won't be swayed by the beliefs of the "collective." You may enjoy helping the unfortunate or taking up causes like environmentalism. You find it easier to communicate through artistic

modes rather than directly. <u>You make decisions based on whether they align with your internal values and dislike conformity.</u> Your question: "What feels right to me?" Authentic, nonjudgmental, supportive.

Choose which of the four types above sounds most like you. Use the two-letter code to identify your type.

My category 2 strength is: _____

Now, which appears to be your primary or dominant strength—the one you use naturally without really thinking? The other is your secondary strength, the one you use often, but have to consciously *decide* to use.

My primary strength is: _____
My secondary strength is: _____

How did you do? Were you surprised by the results of this assessment? Our natural talents can easily remain hidden from us. Through this and the other exercises in this book, you can identify your strengths and learn to use them more strategically to benefit your writing and marketing efforts.

Examples of How to Build on Your Strengths

Let's look at some examples of how you can use your strengths in your writing career based on the eight cognitive functions above. Keep in mind that these are just examples to get you thinking about the many options available to you.

1. **Extroverted Sensing (Se):** Use your adventurous nature to travel to research your novel, create a travel blog, blog about your adventures kayaking or mountain climbing, or establish a new group in your community that regularly explores your local area and reports on events and locations in an online magazine. You may enjoy getting out with other writers to readings or instructional events in your community. Or you may simply blend your love of writing and adventure by hitting the road in a recreational vehicle.

2. **Introverted Sensing (Si):** Apply your organizational skills to create charts, plans, instructions, or recipes for your readers. If you are a history or genealogy buff, you could create blogs around historical topics addressed in your book(s) or host online workshops to share what you learned from your research. You may be perfectly suited to write research papers or memoirs. Writing for a corporation or nonprofit organization may be an ideal fit for you. You may also enjoy traveling to trace the history of your characters or creating family trees to support your stories.

3. **Extroverted Intuiting (Ne):** Your love of brainstorming and experimenting could make you a natural fit for writing "choose your own" adventure stories. Or you could offer your reader background information from your novels. You may be perfectly suited for writing a series, or enjoy creating technical specs for the machines or ships in your books—even give away plans for readers to create these machines at home (out of craft-store materials). You would also make a good

instructor for certain detailed subjects you enjoy and may find that technical writing is right up your alley.

4. **Introverted Intuiting (Ni):** You may feel comfortable creating blogs or nonfiction books that inspire others and be a natural workshop leader and speaker. Using symbols, cards, images, and other tools can help you interpret your intuitive insights or guide others to find theirs. You could use these items in your stories, too, where they might take on symbolic meanings. You might do well expanding your writing services to include graphic design, intuitive work, or coaching. Speech writing may appeal to you, and you're likely to be happy as a freelancer or independent writing entrepreneur.

5. **Extroverted Thinking (Te):** Use your natural talent for organizing and planning to create the perfect book launch or to set up your own system for releasing your three-part book series. Once you have your own process set up for self-publishing, you could offer it to other writers through newsletter freebies or via online or in-person workshops. You could write guest posts or nonfiction books on increasing productivity and efficiency. You may also benefit from creating systems and charts for yourself to keep track of characters, plotlines, deadlines, and publishing schedules.

6. **Extroverted Feeling (Fe):** Use your concern for others to broaden your author platform. Ask yourself: "How can I help others in my areas of interest?" Provide guest posts, free materials, workshops, and more that will help others succeed in various areas, or make it easier for them to solve problems. You may be the perfect person to organize a writers' confer-

ence or retreat, or to create an online fundraising campaign for an independent bookstore. Or just open a bookstore yourself! You'll be perfect at matching people with books.

7. **Introverted Thinking (Ti):** You may enjoy science writing or activities that allow you to solve puzzles and challenging problems. You could write for a think tank or help your readers to troubleshoot problems in a variety of areas, focusing on what interests you. You can offer your readers helpful information on how things work and may particularly enjoy journalism. Perhaps you could run surveys on your blog to gain reader interest and to gather data on a problem you want to solve.

8. **Introverted Feeling (Fi):** You will enjoy writing for causes you care about, which you could do either at a job, with a nonprofit organization or as a freelancer. You can champion your causes by donating funds from the sales of your books while simultaneously gaining reader attention. Expand your platform by highlighting the plights of the downtrodden or by pointing out hypocrisy. Feel free to be a rebel and speak your opinions—you'll find those who agree with you and will follow you.

These are just some fun examples to get your imagination working, so don't feel limited only to what's offered above. Spend some time brainstorming your own ideas on how you can use what you've learned to expand, build, and fine-tune your author platform.

Build on Your Strengths and Use Them to Problem Solve

Building on your strengths involves using a three-step process.

1. **Become aware of the strengths in your life.** Because you may not have been fully aware of your strengths before, the first step is to bring them squarely into your conscious mind. You'll continue to work on doing that through the rest of this book, but for now, based on what you've learned so far, take a step back and observe yourself. Where are you using these strengths in your life? How are you using them? Look for evidence in your daily activities. You can also ask your friends and loved ones to give you feedback.

2. **Start exploring each strength more deeply.** Now that you're aware of your two strongest cognitive processes, it's time to explore them further. Read more about them. Imagine how else you might use them to amplify your writing life. Think about people you know or admire who demonstrate the same strengths and study how they use them. Note how they benefit from them.

3. **Apply your strengths in your daily life.** Once you've explored your strengths—or better yet, while you're exploring them—you can begin to apply what you've learned to your life and your writing career. Here's where you go beyond thinking or reading to engaging in actions that employ these new strengths you've discovered.

Starting today, whenever you set a goal to work on a new writing-related activity, ask yourself: "How can I use my strengths to accomplish this goal more easily?" This can be particularly effective when you have a problem to solve. Here's the basic formula:

My problem is: _____.

I need a solution that makes _____ easier.

I can use my strength to solve this problem in the following way:
_____.

Let's say your problem is that book signings and other public appearances scare you to death. And let's say one of your strengths is extroverted intuiting (Ne). You may follow the formula this way:

My problem is: <u>feeling shy and nervous at public events</u>.

I need a solution that makes <u>public speaking/presenting</u> easier.

I can use my strengths to solve this problem in the following way:

I will use my love of brainstorming to come up with a number of ways I can make public appearances less frightening. I will explore all possible solutions—going in a disguise that fits a character in my book; practicing in front of my friends; signing up for Toastmasters so I can learn how to comfortably speak in public; trying natural, calming herbs or oils that reduce anxiety; getting some counseling on facing my fear; finding ways to focus on the audience instead of myself; etc. Then I will experiment and find the solution that works best for me.

If one of your strengths is introverted feeling (Fi), you may have more success scheduling readings or talks to groups you empathize with, like environmentalists, animal rights groups, people with cancer, or others facing difficulties similar to those your characters face. By tapping into this particular strength, you can use your passion for helping the individual to overcome your own nervousness.

If your strength is extroverted sensing (Se), you may decide to hold your book readings outdoors where you'll be more comfortable or even invite your readers on a short hike where you could answer questions and read from your book once you reach the destination. These sorts of settings may help put you at ease so you feel less "on the spot" and more like you're simply sharing an activity you enjoy with others.

The options are endless. All you need is your imagination.

Make Your Strengths Even Stronger

Building on your strengths is a never-ending endeavor, and trust me, once you start, you'll want to keep doing it, because it's going to be fun for you. Particularly when you use your strengths to support your writing career, you'll find your energy level increasing because writing and perhaps even (gasp!) marketing will be enjoyable!

What are some ways you can continue to improve? Here are a few tips:

1. Engage Your Interests/Passions More Often

Think about those activities you most like to do and do them more often. Find the type of stories you really like to write and write more of those. (It's amazing how many writers try to force themselves into a genre or topic that doesn't work for them.) Use your natural passions to help you in other areas, like marketing.

If you're asking yourself how to build your author platform, ask yourself instead what you're interested in. When you are excited about a topic, your writing and marketing activities involving that topic will be filled with your enthusiasm, and enthusiasm attracts people. Anything you do that involves your interests is likely to be interesting to your readers too.

Ask yourself: "What am I most interested in improving about my author platform?" You may think you *should* create a new website or start a podcast, but if you see a task like this as drudgery, you're not likely to do it well. Ask yourself instead what you're interested in improving and do that. Do you like talking to people? Maybe a podcast is for you. Are you a traveler? Maybe a travel blog would help bring readers to your website. Do you like to do crafts? Maybe some how-to posts would help you find your reading audience.

2. Find Ways to Use Your Strengths to Overcome Weaknesses

Once you know your strengths, you can use them to overcome your weaknesses. Think about those activities you don't do well, or don't enjoy doing. Usually these are areas you struggle in because they don't come naturally to you. First, delegate them if you can. Maybe you can hire someone to redesign your website, for example, or manage your social media accounts.

If delegating is not an option right now, think about how you might use your strength to get around this area of difficulty. Let's say you don't look forward to submitting your work for publication. No one likes facing a potential rejection, and rejection is always a possibility when submitting.

If your strength is Te (extroverted thinking), you can use that strength to make writing your cover letter easier. Perhaps you might review examples of other cover letters, and make your own guidelines on what they usually contain. How do the successful ones begin? How do they end? What key information do they include? Consult some credible resources and create your own query-letter template. Once you finish putting it together, insert your story into it. The best part is you'll have a template you can use for future letters.

This is just one example. If you can tap into your strength to complete a project that you normally dread, you'll not only make the project easier, but you'll develop your strength in a new and unique way while improving on a weakness.

3. Share Your Strengths; Find Ways to Serve Others

Thinking about how you can serve others can be particularly helpful in your writing career. If your strength is introverted sensing (Si), for instance, maybe you can share that strength by helping to preserve your family's memories in a book, video, or other creative project.

If your strength is Ti (introverted thinking), you're good at finding inconsistencies and digging deep to find the truth behind the myth or facade. Maybe you can create a blog that would help save more "gullible" people from making mistakes by warning them of so-called "facts" that may not be so factual, or advising them of steps they can take to protect themselves when traveling, shopping, seeking service providers, or making choices concerning their health.

For this step, ask yourself: "How can I use my strength to serve others?" When you find answers, act on them. Even if they don't directly affect your writing career today, they can help you tremendously in your networking efforts. Everyone remembers the person who wants to help!

4. Focus More on Your Secondary Strength

This is a neat trick I found through my research that can be a lot of fun to try. Check back on your secondary strength. This is the strength that can help take you to ever-higher levels of achievement. Think of it as your secret weapon. Remember your primary strength flows naturally from you. Your secondary strength, however, is one you use by choice. It's time to choose it more often!

Let's say your primary strength is extroverted sensing (Se), and your secondary strength is introverted thinking (Ti). You unconsciously explore new things and seek out stimulation. You don't have to try. But you do have to think about turning inward to contemplate what's happening, to look for inconsistencies, and to find out what makes sense to you.

This secondary strength can be hugely helpful when you're facing a decision or trying to figure out which step you want to take next, but you must make a conscious effort to use it. That may mean setting aside time for a long, thoughtful walk or a drive to allow yourself the space to decompress your thoughts. Scheduling in more time for these types of activities could make life a lot easier for you.

Focus on Strengths Encourages Enthusiasm

Having fun yet? I hope so. The more you explore and use your strengths, usually the more motivated and excited you'll feel about what you're doing, and that's what it's all about. The more fun you're having, the more your enthusiasm will bleed into your work, and the more readers will want to be a part of it.

Discover More:
Employing Your Top Two Cognitive Processes

Look back on your top two cognitive processes. Then brainstorm ways to use one or the other (or both) in the following two areas of your writing career:

1. **I will use my strength in the writing itself** in the following way: (Examples may include creating systems for keeping track of characters, using symbols to show you where the story should go next, and getting out in nature to come up with new story ideas.)

   _____

2. **I will use my strength in my author platform** in the following way: (Examples may include trying a new blogging niche, redesigning the look of your website, using a new tactic on your social media posts, trying different types of guest posts that align with your strengths, starting your own writers' group, and putting together a new freebie for newsletter sign-ups.)

   _____

CHAPTER 9

OWN YOUR STRENGTHS!

WITH ALL THIS talk about strengths, you may be feeling a little uncomfortable. It can be hard to own your talent—to believe you do certain things well. Even when you experience success in the writing world, it can be easy to attribute it to luck or good timing.

Let's dig in to this phenomenon a bit more. Take a moment and choose the best answer for each of the following questions:

1. When I succeed at something related to my writing, I tend to believe it was more because of good timing, hard work, or luck than my own writing ability.
   a. Always
   b. Most of the time
   c. Sometimes
   d. Never

2. When working on a writing project or trying something new related to my creative endeavors, I worry I'm going to fail.
   a. Always

b. Most of the time

c. Sometimes

d. Never

3. When people tell me how talented or creative I am, I'm afraid they've gotten the wrong impression.

a. Always

b. Most of the time

c. Sometimes

d. Never

4. Tests and other forms of evaluation have always made me nervous.

a. Always

b. Most of the time

c. Sometimes

d. Never

5. When someone reads my writing and enjoys it, it feels great, and for a minute I think I might actually be good at this, but that feeling quickly fades and is replaced by other thoughts like *she was just being nice* or *he's not really qualified to judge*.

a. Always

b. Most of the time

c. Sometimes

d. Never

6. When I experience a success with my writing—a good review, an award, or just a finished manuscript—I fear I'll never be able to do it again.

a. Always

    b. Most of the time

    c. Sometimes

    d. Never

7. When I get together with my writing friends or when I attend writing conferences, it seems like everyone else is more talented or gifted than I am.

    a. Always

    b. Most of the time

    c. Sometimes

    d. Never

Scoring: Now add up the number of As, Bs, Cs, and Ds you have:

_____As _____Bs _____Cs _____Ds

Mostly As or Bs: You've likely got a powerful case of imposter syndrome on your hands. **Mostly Cs:** You may struggle with this syndrome now and then, typically when trying something new or stepping out of your comfort zone. **Mostly Ds:** Imposter syndrome may not be a problem for you, but it's worth reading on just in case you encounter it in the future.

Beware of Imposter Syndrome

Imposter syndrome is a condition that was first described by clinical psychologists Pauline Rose Clance and Suzanne Imes in a study published in 1978 in the scientific journal *Psychotherapy Theory, Research, and Practice.* In that study, Clance and Imes described this syndrome as an "internal experience of intellectual phoniness that appears to be particularly prevalent and intense among a select sample of high-achieving women.... Despite outstanding academic and professional accomplishments, women who experience the impostor phenomenon persist in believing that they are really not bright and have fooled anyone who thinks otherwise."

Even when these women racked up numerous achievements in their field—which for most would serve as evidence of legitimacy—these achievements had no effect on their imposter belief. The women credited other factors instead such as luck, timing, personal charm, the ability to meet other's expectations, or hard work.

Early research focused on women, but later studies found this is not a gender-specific issue. In 1993, researchers from Georgia State University reviewed the current scientific literature on the phenomenon and reported the syndrome affected both genders equally, and interestingly enough, self-esteem was not a factor. In other words, a person can have a perfectly healthy self-esteem and still suffer from imposter syndrome. Someone can feel like they're a good and capable person overall, for example, but still have a hard time believing they have what it takes to be a writer.

Researchers discovered other interesting traits about people who suffer from imposter syndrome. They are also more likely to:

- suffer from anxiety

- sway toward the introverted spectrum on the personality scale (Introverts naturally keep important aspects of their personalities hidden from the world—the resulting separation between internal experiences and outward behaviors can give rise to the feelings that the person is not seen for who he or she really is—a main component of imposter syndrome.)

- want to "look good" for others

- come from families with little support or emotional sharing

- be people pleasers

- be perfectionists or workaholics (believing that hard work was necessary to keep up the "façade")

- think everyone around them is smarter and more talented than they are

- discount positive feedback ("She was just being nice.")

- believe their successes are due to something other than their own abilities

- believe that achievement through "hard work" does not reflect true or real ability

- have an adequate self-esteem except in one area of achievement (like writing)

- feel the need to achieve to have a sense of self-worth

- be sensitive to criticism and love praise

- have an ideal image or idealized standard to live up to—and may disregard a performance that doesn't live up to that standard (*Sure, I was a finalist, but I didn't win.*)

- have a fear of failing

- work harder than their peers to "make up" for what they think they lack in intelligence and talent

The Effect of Imposter Syndrome on a Writing Career

Look at the bulleted characteristics above and ask yourself, honestly: How many describe you? I've talked to a lot of writers who struggle with imposter syndrome. All of them wish to overcome it because it's devastating to their careers and emotional well-being. Suffering with this condition means any type of success is never good enough.

"For me, it is all about the imposter syndrome," writes Troy Lambert, freelance writer, editor, author, and blogger, in *Writing and Wellness*. "I live in fear that one of these days, someone will figure out I am not really that good at writing, or I can't really edit because I am not qualified, and I will never land another gig doing either one again."

Just imagine having a story that places in a contest, earns you a coveted publishing contract, garners good reviews, boosts your blog or website success, and leads to workshop and speaking opportunities, or any number of other writing-related accomplishments, but still leaves you feeling like you haven't reached your ideal image of what a "real writer" is. You could suffer from anxiety, depression, burnout, and emotional exhaustion to the point that you eventually abandon your writing career altogether.

Ouch.

Indeed, for these "imposters," success never brings happiness. Instead, it's the opposite as they live in a state of chronic stress, worried their "façade" will fall and they will be "discovered" as the terrible writers they really are!

This fear manifests itself in many ways. Writers may worry about taking on more projects, for fear they will not be able to manage them. They may delay submitting or publishing their work because they fear bad reviews. They quake in their boots when it comes to getting feedback because they're quite certain it will only show what they already suspect—that they have no talent. Worst of all, they fear taking a risk, certain it will not work out. According to early research, this syndrome seems to be more common among those embarking on a new endeavor—perhaps one they don't feel ready to handle.

This spells disaster because writers today have to take risks and learn on their own—often by simply doing. Without the willingness to trust in one's own talent and take a leap of faith now and then, these souls languish behind their keyboards for years getting nowhere.

Overcoming Imposter Syndrome

Fantasy writer Megan Cutler has struggled with imposter syndrome. It convinced her she had to make money from her writing before she could say she was a legitimate writer. This false belief led to her wasting a lot of time doing things that weren't right for her:

> I had convinced myself that I needed to make money to be a *real* writer. I started writing short stories and submitting them to magazines. I felt like I needed validation to prove that I could make it, that a single sale would indicate I had the talent needed to succeed. It was foolish. I don't even like writing short stories! Yet I regarded every rejection as a sign that I was doomed to fail.

Megan kept at it until she finally had a moment of clarity after reading *The Alchemist* by Paulo Coelho and understood that she had given up her personal power.

> I had given up my agency. I had put power over my passions into the hands of unknown, unseen strangers. I had

allowed fear of failure to bar the way. So I made a decision to take control. I could choose the method by which I shared my work. My decisions could shape my journey. And I have never allowed myself to forget that.

That's when Megan started self-publishing and she's never looked back. To date she's published five novels (and several short stories!) and is a much happier and more fulfilled writer. She found a way to recalculate her writer's journey in a direction that works for her.

> When people ask me if I would still write if I never managed to be successful, my answer is always yes. I have tried not writing; it doesn't work for me. It's like trying to hold my breath forever. Eventually, my brain forces me back to the page.

Sometimes imposter syndrome comes and goes during a writer's career, but sometimes it's a constant companion. Such is the case for Troy. "Intellectually," he writes, "I know I am good at what I do, from fiction and technical writing and research to content marketing and business. But at some point in nearly every day, emotionally I doubt my competence, and no number of endorsements on my LinkedIn profile or the sheer number of novels, articles, and reports I have written will convince me otherwise."

Troy never stops working to keep imposter syndrome at bay, employing activities such as regular exercise, yoga, and meditation. His latest project is a book on the business of writing, for which he's perfectly suited. (Keep an eye out for it. Find out more about Troy and all the other authors featured here in the Featured Writers section at the back of this book.)

You may have a similar story of how imposter syndrome has filled you with doubt and lured you off your course. As you can see, you're not alone in your struggle. The important thing is to get back on track quickly once you realize what's happening.

Dumping the Imposter

How do you dump this destructive syndrome? First of all, consider talking with a therapist. Studies have shown because the imposter syndrome can have its roots in childhood experiences, it often helps to get to the core of those experiences with a trained professional who can give you the tools you need to grow beyond them. In addition to therapy, there are other methods you can try to help you boost your confidence and own your strengths.

1. Remember: You're not alone.

Actress Emma Watson and author Neil Gaiman have both publicly admitted to experiencing imposter syndrome. Neil Gaiman famously stated in his University of the Arts commencement speech: "The first problem of any kind of even limited success is the unshakable conviction that you are getting away with something and that any moment now they will discover you. It's impostor syndrome, something my wife Amanda christened the Fraud Police." And while acting in the Harry Potter movies, Emma Watson stated, "Any moment, someone's going to find out I'm a total fraud. I can't possibly live up to what everyone thinks I am."

Imposter syndrome is common in every walk of life. Remind yourself that you, like so many others, have the power to lessen this syndrome's effect on your life and your writing career.

2. Accept that writing careers fluctuate.

Every writer, no matter how successful, goes through ups and downs. Even if you do everything "right" and possess extreme natural talent and intelligence, things can still go wrong. Then again, sometimes they'll go incredibly right. Both situations can exacerbate the imposter syndrome. When things go wrong you blame yourself, and when things go right you assume it was all a fluke and that time will ferret out the truth about your lack of skills.

Chasing after some ideal writing life (that ideal image that imposter syndrome creates) will only leave you disappointed and depressed. Develop a more realistic view of the writer's journey. Imagine a trip across country. The car may break down in some unknown place. You may eat out and develop food poisoning. You could end up in a hotel that has paper-thin walls. You could be delayed by bad weather.

At the same time you may see views that astound you, meet amazing people, and have some of the most fun and life-changing experiences of your life. A writing career is like that—sometimes good, sometimes lousy. Let go of the ideal image. Allow your experience to be as it will without judging yourself so harshly.

3. Develop a commitment to service in your work.

Personally, I've found this to be one of the most successful ways to deal with imposter syndrome, anxiety, and all the other negative states we writers often go through. Try seeing what you do—all facets of your writing endeavors—as your way of living in service to others.

Anytime you step back and say, "What is the work asking of me at this point?" it's amazing how quickly your feelings of despair and imposterism can vanish, often to be replaced with solutions presented by your creative mind. Every time you step back and ask yourself, "How can I use my skills to benefit others?" you unlock your creative imagination and allow it to go to work for you.

Try it. The next time you imagine you're a fraud and are soon to be found out, take the focus off yourself and put it on others. I'm not saying go do the dishes or make dinner for your friends. Use your writing-related skills to be of service either to the writing itself or, through your writing, to other people.

4. Recognize the predictable pattern imposter syndrome takes.

Even if imposter syndrome is a constant companion on your writing journey, chances are it shows up at predictable times, so you can be ready. Of course, the timing may not be great. Usually it's when you want to try something new, particularly if you are "crossing over" into an area where you haven't had any achievements yet.

Let's say you've been a successful romance writer, but now you'd like to cross over into nonfiction. Expect imposter syndrome to show up. You haven't written nonfiction before, so you're clearly not an expert. Who are you to try this?

This can also happen if you realize after the fact that you need to learn a new skill. If you publish a book, but it doesn't sell well, you may feel shame about that, not realizing that marketing is an entirely new skill you need to develop. It's not about you "not having what it takes," but simply about learning to do something new you haven't tried before.

The quicker you recognize the pattern, the more likely you'll be able to diminish its effect. "Okay, this is normal. I'm trying something new, but I can learn how to do this. I can figure it out."

5. Accept imposter syndrome as a good sign.

Instead of worrying about people discovering you're a fraud, use these feelings as a signal that you're doing something right. They often show up when you're challenging yourself with a new project, which is great! Though it may not feel so good at the moment, it's the only way to grow and improve.

Discover More:
Journal Your Way Out of Imposter Syndrome

Think about when you've felt the presence of imposter syndrome. Choose one of the following questions and journal about it. Dig deep and try to root out what's causing it, because once you understand where it's coming from, you'll be more likely to lessen its power over you.

1. When do you first remember feeling like an imposter? Can you zero in on the action or activity that triggered those feelings?

2. Are you a people pleaser? What is your earliest memory of feeling like you had to please others to be accepted?

3. Do you feel like you need to prove to someone you are worthy or good enough? Who is that person? When did you first feel like this? Can you let go of these feelings?

4. Are you avoiding new activities in your writing career because you feel you don't have what it takes? What would you do if you could eliminate that fear?

5. If you remove your mask, what do you fear will happen? Are you concerned you'll disappoint someone?

6. Think back on your last achievement as a writer. Maybe you got a story published, finished writing a novel, redesigned your website, were a finalist in a contest ... anything. Were you proud of yourself at the time, or

did you feel like you had just gotten lucky? Describe the experience. Can you see that you did deserve credit even if you can't accept it?

7. Why do you write? Do you feel it is your best way to be of use in the world? Does it feel connected to your purpose? Do you feel an intense desire to get your story out into the world? Write down your reasons why and then ask yourself: "What if my next project totally flops, how will I feel? Can I simply enjoy the process of doing something challenging without worrying about success or failure?"

CHAPTER 10

POWER UP YOUR PLATFORM

O NE OF THE first times I ever felt powerful was when my kindergarten teacher called on me to read a book passage in class. I was a shy little girl and the other kids intimidated me, but reading, I could do. My mom had taught me how before I ever stepped foot in a school, and I loved it. I would beg her to take me to the library every week as I was gobbling up books like they were donuts, and I always needed more when the week was over.

So when the teacher asked me to read, I could feel the words falling easily from my lips, my voice confident and even, and more than that, I could hear the other kids listening. No one was staring, no one was mocking—they were just listening to the story. In those few moments, I felt powerful.

In our culture, the word *power* is often used in a negative context, as we often focus on those who use it to limit or harm others. But if you look up the definition in the Merriam-Webster's Collegiate Dictionary, the first meaning you'll read is, "to be able; ability to act or produce an effect." In other words, *power* is a skill or strength.

The second meaning reads: "possession of control, authority, or influence over others." Combine those first two meanings and you have exactly what a writer needs to build a successful platform: the ability to act and produce an effect that allows you to influence others.

So the question then becomes: Where are you gaining power?

Personal Power

If I were to ask you to share one time when you witnessed someone fully in his or her power, what would you tell me? Would you talk about the rock star who seemed to have endless energy while holding the audience in the palm of his hand? Would you tell about your child's classroom teacher who managed to get her students excited about learning division, mainly because she acted so excited herself? Would you wax nostalgic about the time your father built an entire cabin with his own two hands?

What does it mean to feel personal power? There are many ways to describe it, but for now, I'm talking about those times in life when, while you're doing an activity, you feel like you're vibrating at your highest frequency. You have boundless energy, you're excited, and you're able to accomplish what you're doing with ease. When you look back on the experience, you can't wait to do it again.

But you can't be powerful alone—you need others. You discover your power when you become aware of that thing you do that not only puts you in your highest vibration, but also causes others to respond with enthusiasm. Personal power draws others to you, and the more you use it, the more your platform grows.

In other words, even if you feel energetic and excited while riding your bike, if you're not influencing others, that's not the power we're talking about. If, however, you're riding your bike through town and stopping to show others how you've souped-up the motor, and maybe you even allow them to take it for a spin, and then you give them a bookmark that advertises your *Soup-Up Your Bike* book, and people respond positively to your visits, then this sort of community outreach is part of your personal power.

This isn't about coercing or gaining authority over others. It's about engaging them so they can't help but pay attention to what you're doing, hopefully enough that they will want to buy your book or your course or whatever else you may be offering.

Finding Personal Power

Once you find your personal power, you can use it to guide your writing career forward. Take Laurie Buchanan, PhD, for instance. When her mother was only thirty-three years old, she died of breast cancer.

"I was dismayed," Laurie wrote on *Writing and Wellness*, "no, *shocked* at what traditional medicine did, and failed to do, for people in her position. In my heart of hearts it seemed there *must* be something more."

Inspired to take action on behalf of her mother's memory, Laurie studied holistic health and energy medicine, or what is sometimes called "integrative medicine" or "complementary care." She was board certified by the American Association of Drugless Practitioners and became a holistic health practitioner.

"With what I learned," she wrote, "I created a nine-month experience for my clients called *Life Harmony*. I created this program for clients who knew they needed to change, but didn't know how. The

Life Harmony experience is a 'guidepost' of sorts; a way show-er. It's designed to help people turn intention into action and bridge the gap between where they are and where they want to be—body, mind, and spirit."

At the time, Laurie had no intention of writing a book. She simply wanted to teach others what she had learned, so they could live healthier, happier lives. That was her personal power—inspiring others to make positive changes. But soon, some of her clients suggested she get her ideas down in a more permanent way.

"The curriculum I wrote for this experience is relevant, engaging, and actionable, and my clients said: 'This needs to be a book!'"

It wasn't an easy task. Sometimes, Laurie felt like giving up. In the end, her book *Note to Self* was published and won several book awards. The positive reception bolstered Laurie's confidence and compelled her to keep going. Obviously, what she was doing was succeeding—she was gaining power in the arena she had chosen. She recently published her second book, *The Business of Being*, which blends business and spirituality and shows readers how to "thrive, soul-side out, in and out of the workplace."

Had Laurie failed to listen to the feedback she was getting from her clients, she might never have created a course, written a book, or found her true purpose, which she believes is to "leave the slightest footprint on the planet, while at the same time making a lasting impression on its inhabitants—one that's positive, uplifting, constructive, and healing."

Every creative artist has a similar power inside. The trick is to find it. Once you do, you'll know it, as people will start responding and you'll get that positive feedback you're looking for.

Personal Power Helps Writers Market Their Work

Finding personal power is particularly important to you as a writer because it guides you toward how to market your work. You may believe you don't possess any such power or strength, because you're introverted or you don't really like marketing or you'd rather not influence people, but you'd be shortchanging yourself.

We all like connecting with others through activities we're passionate about. You may be introverted, but get you talking about one of your favorite subjects, and I'll bet you become animated and energetic. You may think you have no desire to influence people, but what if I said you could help people through your personal power? Would that change things?

A Formula for Finding Your Personal Contributions

For the rest of this chapter, I'll be guiding you through some exercises to help you find your personal power and thus, discover new ways to connect with people and spread the word about the creative work you're doing. We're going to start with a formula that uses your talents and passions to reveal your personal contributions—those activities you can then employ to expand your personal power and get noticed.

Start by answering the following questions in your journal:

Talent

Think back to a time when someone came to you and said something like, "You're good at this. Can you help me?" What were they talking about? For what knowledge, skills, and gifts do others seek you out?

Likely, writing is one of them, but try to go beyond that. Writing what? And what else do people ask you for? Do they ask you to teach them something, support them, complete some sort of task for them, talk to someone else for them, give them advice about a situation, or figure out something complex? Write down what comes to mind.

Now think back to a time when someone patted you on the back and told you "good job" or a time when others supported you or encouraged a particular thing you had done. What was that thing? What do you do that others are impressed with?

When you're finished with these questions, you should have at least four talents written down.

Passion

Now shine the light on your own passions. Name those activities that when you're doing them, time seems to fly by. What activities most energize you or engage you? What challenges do you love to take on? Again, these can include writing, but it helps to be more specific, so define the types of writing and then go beyond and describe the other activities you're passionate about.

Examples may include gardening, teaching or coaching, athletics, travel adventures, community building, cooking, flying or any other type of skill-based activity, horseback riding, ranching, research, music making, artwork, carpentry … the list goes on. Choose at least four of your passions and write them down in your journal.

Contribution

Now it's time to marry talent with passion to figure out where your personal power is and how you may influence others. The formula goes like this: simply write down one of your talents, choose a passion (from those you discovered above), and then come up with the obvious contribution the two can accomplish when combined. Here are a few examples:

Talent	Passion	Contribution
Teaching	Flying	Teaching others to fly
Painting	Traveling	Painting pictures of places you travel to
Knitting	Reading	Starting "knitting book clubs"
Singing	Fitness	Creating a musical fitness program

If you don't find an obvious contribution right away, give it more thought and play around with the combinations to see what you come up with. For instance, using the examples above, I could come up with other entirely new contributions:

Talent	Passion	Contribution
Teaching	Traveling	Teaching others how to travel easily, or teaching them about traveling to different locations and what to find there
Painting	Fitness	Painting pictures of different types of exercises, or creating a new "walk and paint" program for people who want to explore creativity in a healthy setting
Knitting	Flying	This is a tough one, but use your imagination—perhaps you can create designs for knitted items one can use while on the plane, or share tips for how to take your knitting with you when traveling
Singing	Reading	Hmm … maybe recommend good books about singing, or turn your own children's stories into songs for kids

Remember—you can apply any of these contributions to your author platform. We'll talk more about that below. The key to this exercise is to find interesting combinations that will attract people and make them sit up and go, "Oh, that's cool!"

Now it's your turn. Combine the talents and passions you recorded into various combinations and see what contributions evolve. Feel free to play with this for a few minutes. Shuffle your pairings around, or add new talents and passions as they come to mind. Brainstorm how they might be combined into a contribution that truly excites you.

Talent	Passion	Contribution

The Final Step: Figuring Out How to Use Your Contribution in Your Author Platform

Once you fill out the formula above, you have only one step left to complete: How will you use this in your author platform? This is actually the fun part. Let's expand on the original examples:

Contribution	Author Platform
Teaching others to fly	New blog with weekly tips on "how to fly" or "flying smarter," book signings at the airport, airplanes on all author swag
Painting pictures of places you've traveled	A travel blog that includes the paintings, or perhaps details on the process used in painting the images; free reports that explain how the settings from the paintings relate to the settings in the author's books; including the paintings in the actual books; conducting a live painting at a book signing
Starting "knitting book clubs"	Holding knitting events for each book club in which the author conducts a reading, offering patterns for knitting projects that characters make in the books, blogging about great knitting books (with book reviews), creating an online knitting book club, connecting with other knitting book clubs
Creating a musical fitness program	A fitness blog about all the ways music can help one become healthier, through listening, singing or playing; incorporating mini-musical workouts at book signings and events; offering video instruction on fitness; creating a DVD of an original musical workout that is sold along with a book

You can personalize these even more depending on the type of writing you do. In the first example, the writer might create a blog solely about airplanes—different types of aircraft, history of airplanes, and various design elements. If he writes in the suspense genre, then maybe he focuses on flights gone wrong and details on various accidents and crash reports. Or if he's a science fiction writer, maybe he blogs about planes and UFO sightings, or about new shuttle designs that incorporate advanced technology, making space travel more accessible. If he's a romance writer, maybe he blogs about people flying to romantic places in their small, personal-use planes, and then maybe he holds book signings at these locations!

In the second example, the writer could incorporate poetry with her paintings, including painting the verse on the actual canvas or even creating an art book with her paintings and poems. If she's a romance writer, she could offer her painting services to others, perhaps for weddings or reunions; use her own paintings on her covers; or create a painting and give it away in a contest on her website. If she's a fantasy writer, she could create paintings of her settings or characters and hold a contest for her readers to see who could identify all the characters in the painting.

Let's try another example.

Drawing + Working with Children = Inspiring Children with Positive Messages
(Talent)   (Passion)   (Contribution)

Imagine a writer who's enjoyed drawing all her life, and also loves creating happy, positive stories that uplift the reader. How might she use this contribution in her author marketing? We don't have to look any further than Cindy Helms, an artist who's done just that.

"Ever since I can remember," Cindy wrote in her *Writing and Wellness* interview, "from as early as first grade, I had been preoccupied with coloring, art, making up stories, and journaling." But Cindy had what she called a "tumultuous" childhood, and for years her journals were filled with her troubles. When she went back and read through them, she was "depressed to an unprecedented degree.

Everything I read sounded like a frustrated, disillusioned, complaining, warped broken record. Over and over again I wrote the same things. Different year. Same issues. I was appalled."

So Cindy banned herself from journaling and conducted her own experiment: "I let myself have one sheet of 9 x 12 paper at a time. On this paper I could write no words, only images. The images had to be funny, cute, silly, creative, colorful, unique, uplifting, or energetic. If I felt good after I finished with a piece of paper, then the paper would go into a box."

Soon she had collected hundreds of drawings. "My kids and my husband loved it. They saw how happy I was every time I added a new drawing. They started inquiring about what came to be known as Mama's drawing-of-the-day."

No doubt, Cindy had found her personal power. Already she was connecting with and influencing others, even if they were only in her immediate family. Her husband encouraged her to turn the drawings into stories, and she agreed, but then tragedy hit.

"I wrote stories and paired them up with the characters I had drawn. I made book dummies and sent them out to publishers. I enrolled in design classes at a community college ... I was motivated. And then my husband died. Suddenly. He was forty-five years old. I was forty-four, and our boys were eleven and fourteen."

For a long time Cindy had no energy for her stories. "But I knew I had to create a children's book if only because my husband had believed in me. I had to do it as a memorial for him. As healing for me ... as proof to my kids that our life could go on."

She knew she couldn't accomplish her goal alone, so she got some help. "I hired a book consultant and an online marketing expert. I attended publishing seminars. I took classes in Adobe Photoshop, InDesign, and Illustrator. I looked for mentors and coaches everywhere I could find them. I studied children's books and spent hours in the library and bookstores, as I had done when my boys were young. I talked with teachers and librarians. I set a budget, a project plan, and deadlines. I shared my goals with friends, who then would check in to see how things were going. I spent money where it made sense but tried to do for myself the things that fit my interests and abilities."

Soon Cindy reached her goal of publishing a children's book, and since then she's published several more. No matter what happens, she loves the work, which is another clue that she's found her personal power.

"I let go of my need to control people's responses and learned not to be driven by other opinions. There is no need to wait for tragedy to make this switch. There is no reason to horde our creativity when there is so much of it lacking in the world. Throw it out there into great conversation and see just how much it will contribute. The surprises that come about are so much better than the fear that isolates."

Five Types of Personal Power

I encourage you to play with the talent + passion formula and see what you come up with. Carry each scenario around with you for a day or two and see how it feels, and then try another one. Keep matching your talents with your passions to come up with contributions and eventually the right one will stick.

Meanwhile, let's talk about other ways to grow your personal power. As a creative entrepreneur, you'll need to become more powerful in several distinct areas, as it will make achieving your goals easier. Here are the five most important personal powers as well as ideas for how you might gain influence in each.

1. Expert Power

How well do you know your stuff? The more educated and knowledgeable you are about your niche, the more you'll be able to help those who come to you for information or assistance. The key is to build your status as the expert who's able to give others something of value.

This doesn't mean you have to *be* an expert straight out of the gate. Once you choose your author theme or platform niche, you can easily educate yourself little by little until you *are* that expert. The more you research, blog, and share what you're learning, the more of an expert you will become and the more confidence you'll have.

Also think about the areas where you are already an expert. Most of us have areas where we've developed skills and honed talents. If you choose one of these areas for your niche, it will be even easier to continue to develop those skills to expert level.

Tips for Growing Expert Power

- Keep taking classes, reading books, and going to conferences. Keep learning!

- Write and publish in your expert area—not only on your website and blog, but on other blogs, in magazines and journals, in your local paper, etc.

- Teach your skills to others through blogging, online courses, magazine articles, in-person workshops, books, in the schools, through community education, etc.

2. Network Power

Who do you know? Networking is important to you as an author if you want to get noticed and sell your books and other products. The more people you know in the writing and publishing worlds—and in the world of your niche—the bigger your sphere of influence, which helps you gain power.

I've interviewed over 250 writers on *Writing and Wellness*, and just about every one of them talks about how you can't succeed in this business alone. You need help. Others can inspire and motivate you. They can also open doors for you, alert you to new opportunities, introduce you to others who could help propel your career forward, and more.

Tips for Growing Network Power

- Attend at least one writing event (preferably more) per year—a conference, writing retreat, writing workshop, etc. Meet other writers and teachers face-to-face. It's one of the best ways you can network!

- Connect with other writers, editors, agents, and publishers online through your social media networks.

- Guest post regularly! Find other blogs in your niche and send them well-crafted queries and posts.

- Reach out in your home community. Teach a workshop, host an event, or contribute to some sort of activity that fits within your niche.

- Follow through on your communications, and treat all your contacts with the utmost respect. Do what you say you're going to do, and don't be afraid to help others out for free now and then.

3. Physical Power

How much power emanates from your physical being? Are you energetic and motivated or tired and apathetic? Are you strong and resilient or do you tend to shrink away from challenges? Your desire to grow your power will go nowhere if your body doesn't cooperate.

Even if you're battling a difficult disease or illness right now, you can increase your physical power through small changes in your daily habits. There's no way around it—physical energy is of utmost importance if we expect to succeed in this writing gig, and energy comes from good nutrition, regular exercise, daily stress relief, and consistent sleep habits.

Tips for Growing Physical Power

- Evaluate how you feel right now. If you're not waking up full of energy and ready to go, try to figure out what's hindering you.

- Make sure you're eating healthy meals and exercising at least thirty minutes a day, plus getting the recommended seven-to-eight hours of sleep per night. If any of these are missing, your physical power will dwindle.

- Partner up with other people who have lots of energy and stamina. They will rub off on you!

- Practice disciplined self-care every day—do what's best for your body and mind!

4. Interpersonal Power

How do you relate to others when you're around them? This can obviously affect your power to connect with or influence them, right? If you're likeable, persuasive, and charismatic, you're going to have better luck getting people to listen to you and to potentially buy into what you're selling, so to speak.

This one can be particularly difficult for many who prefer to be home alone writing rather than out communicating with others. But remember, we're talking about growing your tribe here. We want people to pay attention to the work you're doing. Speaking as a die-hard introvert who is reserved and shy, I can confidently say, you can learn these skills if you put your mind to it.

Tips for Growing Interpersonal Power

- Learn more about it. Read books and take classes on communication, public speaking, body language, or overcoming shyness. Think of "communicating with others" as a skill you can learn, because that's just what it is—it's no different than learning to ski or play the piano.

- Always focus more on the other person than on yourself. Ask questions and turn your attention to getting to know him or her. If you're genuinely interested in others, they'll be interested in you.

- Practice good posture. Simply standing up straight helps you look and feel more confident.

- Be present in the moment. Make eye contact. Focus on where you are and on the conversation you're having. Don't allow your mind to drift to other things like how tired you are or how you hope to leave soon.

- Look your best. It will not only help you feel more confident, it will cause others to view you with respect.

5. Image Power

What kind of image are you projecting, not only in person, but online? What image do others form of you based on your photos, texts, stories, or posts? You can project personal power if you look like you know what you're doing—if your website is organized, your social media posts are on brand (on theme), and your graphics look professional. Ask your friends to take a look at your platforms. Is it clear within a few seconds what you're all about? If so, you'll have a better chance of retaining a viewer's attention—and of eventually selling him or her a book or other creative project.

Like it or not, our online world is fast-paced and visual. A reader will come to your website or social media channel and decide within a few seconds whether he or she wants to stay and look around, based on the type of image you project.

The Nielsen Norman Group, a technological research group, states that users often leave web pages within ten-to-twenty seconds, unless you have a strong value to offer them. That means if your site is subpar with poor images and confusing navigation, you're going to lose your reader before he or she even gets to your books.

Tips for Growing Image Power

- Realize that everything you do online affects your image. Be purposeful about the posts, pictures, and other things you put up, and try to stay consistent with your author theme.

- As you gain more experience and build your expertise, update your website and social media platforms to reflect your progress.

- Consider getting professional author photos taken. Your photo will appear in multiple places—on your books, websites, social media platforms, flyers advertising your events, etc. It's important for it to accurately reflect your accomplishments.

- Work on having your image reflect your author theme. If you're all about romance, for example, keep that consistent across your online platforms in your posts, images, and graphics. In other words, as a cowboy romance writer, you may have more horse and rider images across your sites, with accompanying earthy colors, whereas if you're a thriller writer, you may have more urban images with darker colors.

Listen to Feedback and Follow It

By remaining open to feedback from others, you may find you have strengths you didn't even realize you had. Maybe people love your workshops, for example, but you didn't really think of yourself as a teacher. That's okay—go with it. Listen to that feedback, follow it, and then listen some more.

Or maybe people like your fiction, but they're super-nuts about your nonfiction. That doesn't mean you should stop writing fiction, but you should pay attention to that feedback and use it to build your career. Maybe you're really good with kids and find that you're getting some great feedback about your visits with them in schools or libraries. Maybe you're a passionate advocate for a certain cause, and the people involved in that cause want you to do more.

The world will give you clues as to which direction you should go. Keep trying new things, and listen to the feedback. It will help you find where you're gaining power, after which you can focus more on building those areas.

Discover More: Where Are You Gaining Power?

Think back over your creative pursuits in the last year. Try to remember when someone responded positively to something you were doing. It may have been that they liked a piece you wrote or an activity you performed. Write down the details in your journal, answering the following questions:

- What activity was I doing, or what writing piece was it?

- What did the person say? (Recall as much as you can.)

- What was the "theme" behind what I was doing? (What was the idea behind it? Were you teaching, throwing a party, coaching, advocating for something, encouraging or motivating others, building something, entertaining, or something else?)

- How did you feel while you were doing it?

Looking back over your answers, does this activity reflect a strength of yours? If so, write down the strength in the area where you've been keeping track of your strengths, if it's not already there. If you have already written it down and it showed up again here, take note that this is one of your more prominent strengths.

Now ask yourself: "When doing this activity, was I using my talent and passion to influence others?" If so—or if you could use this sort of activity in that way—write that down for future reference.

CHAPTER 11

CREATE YOUR
AUTHOR THEME

WHEN YOU SEE a McDonald's sign, do you think of cheap, fast food that tastes good? Recognizable brand names have the ability to bring up specific, concrete ideas in your mind. When you see a Domino's sign, a Nike swoosh, or an Apple label, you know exactly what you can expect from these companies' products. That's because they've invested significant time and energy into creating images and statements to convey those messages to you. So when you see the Nike logo or read the tagline "Just do it," you immediately think of Nike sportswear.

As a writer, you're a business owner who has books, stories, blogs, courses, etc. as products to sell. Much like any other business, a writing business needs messaging—a logo, a tagline, and a mission statement—to convey the appropriate marketing message to readers. But you can't develop these types of messaging materials until you discover your own author theme.

A theme is a central marketing idea or message that communicates to readers what your products are all about. It focuses on your customer and presents in clear terms what they can expect from you. So instead of saying, "I write sexy science fiction books," you turn it around to focus on the consumer's point of view and say something like, "Sexy science fiction that gets your heart racing."

Developing a business theme also helps you as a writer. It's an effective way to determine what you stand for. It also gives you a more focused vision, which will allow you to create effective strategies and goals for your future. With a theme, you can create clear objectives rather than simply muddling through your marketing efforts.

In this two-part chapter you'll learn about finding your theme not only as a writer, but as a marketer. In today's writing world, it's imperative to figure out what lane you're traveling in. Even if you think you've found your lane, you still need to firmly establish your theme across your entire author platform—including your writing, website, social media, newsletter, book swag, and the rest. Helping people understand exactly what to expect from you by aligning the image you present across everything you do helps you reach more readers, which is the goal.

Part I: Digging for Your Author Theme

The good news is the clues to your unique niche as a writer are already in your life, you just need to know where to find them and then how to interpret them. To do this, begin by answering the questions listed below. Note these may not make sense to you at first, but stick with them, and they will reveal your true creative self, which will in turn direct you to your author theme. Grab your notebook or journal and off you go.

Your Author Heroes

List at least four of your author heroes. It's okay to use the ones you listed in chapter seven, or if you didn't list enough there, you can add to that list now. These should be writers you've admired for years, that you regularly read because you love their work so much. Write down each person's name and then what you love most about their work. Try to limit your explanation to one or two words.

Here's an example:

Author hero #1: Margaret Atwood
Why I love her: Descriptive prose

It may be hard to select just one thing you like about each author, but it's important you limit it for our purposes later on.

Author hero #1: _____
Why I love him/her: _____

Author hero #2: _____
Why I love him/her: _____

Author hero #3: _____
Why I love him/her: _____

Author hero #4: _____
Why I love him/her: _____

Your Music Heroes

There is a lot of crossover in the creative arts, and I've found many of my heroes I admire in the music world have similar qualities to those I admire in the writing world. You, too, may be surprised at the parallels between the reasons you like certain musicians/singers/songwriters and favorite authors.

As you did with your author heroes, list four of your musical heroes and then provide one reason why you like each one. Again, limit your descriptions to a few words.

Music hero #1: _____

Why I love him/her: _____

Music hero #2: _____

Why I love him/her: _____

Music hero #3: _____

Why I love him/her: _____

Music hero #4: _____

Why I love him/her: _____

Funeral Songs

Do you feel like you're filling out a dating app? Hang with me here! Below, list the three songs you'd like to have played at your funeral, and explain in a few words why you'd include each one. I'm not being morbid, but it's a good way to get you thinking about the songs you think truly represent who you are and your life-view.

In other words, don't put down the songs you think your family would like or that would allow everyone to have a good time, but choose those you think reflect the essence of you.

Song #1: _____

Why I'd include it: _____

Song #2: _____

Why I'd include it: _____

Song #3: _____

Why I'd include it: _____

Your Road Trip Thoughts

Now imagine yourself driving on a long road trip and everyone else in the car is asleep. You have a long way to go and you can't turn on the radio as you'll wake everyone up. With only your own thoughts to entertain you, what would you think about? Again, don't get too analytical here, just think about the three things you'd most likely or usually reflect on when you're driving. You'll write each of these topics in the form of a question. Here are some examples:

Where will technology be in ten years?

Is there really a purpose to life?

Wouldn't it be cool if a UFO appeared right now?

Will so-and-so get together with what's his face?

How can I improve my life for my family?

What would my life be like if I were a (spy, president of the United States, supermodel, etc.)?

Okay, your turn. Remember—in the form of a question.

Thought #1: _____

Thought #2: _____

Thought #3: _____

Book Turn-Offs

Think about all those times when you started reading a new book only to quickly grow frustrated with it. Maybe you kept reading anyway, or perhaps you put it down and never picked it up again. Think about what it was that caused you to feel that way. Maybe you were bored, or the book wasn't as interesting as you hoped it would be, or the author's style turned you off.

I lose interest the moment I can tell the book is formulaic. If I can generally predict what's going to happen, the act of reading becomes a chore rather than a pleasure.

What three things can cause you to put a book down? Be succinct in your explanations.

Turn-off #1: _____

Turn-off #2: _____

Turn-off #3: _____

Part II: Excavating Your "Author Theme" from Your Answers

It's now time to move on to the second part of this chapter where you analyze all your answers and start connecting the dots. Take the "whys" from each of the first three exercises (author heroes, music heroes, and songs) and put them together. You should have something that looks like this:

Author Heroes

Fast-paced stories

Futuristic settings

Action oriented

Always ends well

Music Heroes

The music is exciting!

Gives me an escape

Makes me want to dance

Reflects the truths in life

Funeral Songs

It's about loving life

It's about standing up for what you believe in

It expresses love for family

It's about being strong and resilient

Add your answers to the other two questions—thoughts while driving and book turn-offs. Continuing the example:

Thoughts While Driving

Where will technology be in ten years?

Is there really a purpose to life?

Wouldn't it be cool if a UFO showed up right now?

Book Turn-Offs

Predictable endings

Shallow characters

Boring scenes

Now imagine yourself taking a bird's-eye view of what you're seeing. From this vantage point, what themes are emerging? What commonalities do you notice in your answers? I'll help you more with this in a moment, but first, let me explain why these types of exercises are helpful.

You Don't Know Yourself As Well As You Think You Do

You've probably heard that what we see in the world is really a reflection of who we are. The authors you admire, for example, are your heroes because some part of them or their work reflects some part of you. It's not that you're just like them or that your work will be exactly like theirs, but more that some part of what they're doing resonates with you. As you become aware of what you notice in the world, you'll also begin to better understand yourself and where you want to go as an artist.

This step is crucial because we need to know ourselves well enough to plot our writing careers, and research shows we often don't know ourselves well at all! In a review of sixteen studies involving thousands of employees, scientists found that a person's coworkers were much better at recognizing how that person's personality would affect his job performance than the person himself was.

In another study, researchers found that while people had good insight into their own emotional stability, their friends were better at predicting their performance on an IQ test or *creativity* test!

It is hard to be objective about ourselves, particularly our creativity. This mysterious characteristic that surfaces through our stories and other projects is difficult to define in a way that communicates what we're all about to our readers. We usually draw a blank because we don't really know what it is we're all about. This can be a problem when trying to build a writing career that requires you to communicate clearly to readers exactly what they'll discover when they open your book or check out your blog.

The key to establishing a good fan base is to find your "tribe," the people who fit with your type of creativity. Of course, it's a lot harder to find them if you don't know your own type of yourself!

The "Find Your Author Theme" Formula

Let me begin with a disclaimer: a paint-by-number method for finding your author theme doesn't exist. You have to continue to explore, experiment, and reflect to get one that accurately defines you. I can help you get started, though, with this fun exercise.

Three-Word Author Theme Exercise

Looking at the list you generated from all your answers, you're going to create a new list of single words. Simply adjust each phrase or answer so it's reflected in one word. I've got some examples for you.

Note: When considering your answers for what turns you off about a book, choose a word that reflects the *opposite*—so your word describes what would keep you reading.

Answer	One-word Statement
Fast-paced stories	Fast-paced
Futuristic settings	Futuristic
Action oriented	Action or Active
Always ends well	Optimistic

The music is exciting!	Exciting
Gives me an escape	Escape
Makes me want to dance	Movement
Talks about life	Life
It's about loving life	Vitality
It's about standing up for what you believe in	Courage
It expresses love for family	Family
It's about being strong and resilient	Resilience
Where will technology be in ten years?	Technology
Is there really a purpose to life?	Purpose
Wouldn't it be cool if a UFO showed up right now?	Otherworldly
Predictable endings	*Unpredictable*
Shallow characters	*Deep*
Boring scenes	*Captivating*

Now look at the list on the right column and pick out the top three words that appeal to you most. These are words that energize you when you think about them. Use these three words to create a sentence, which will lay the foundation for your author theme. Choose those three words now:

1: _____

2: _____

3: _____

Insert each word into the following sentence in whatever order you like. The sentence won't make sense yet; that's okay. Just insert the words for now.

I write _____ (word 1) stories about _____ (word 2) that help people _____ (word 3).

Let's try an example. Say you choose the following three words from the list:

1. Fast-paced
2. Optimistic
3. Otherworldly

So the sentence might read:

I write fast-paced stories about otherworldly that help people optimistic.

Now we can rework this a bit so it makes sense:

I write fast-paced stories about otherworldly creatures that help people feel optimistic about life.

You can see potential for an author theme there, right? Take that statement now and narrow it down to create some taglines you could use in your marketing messaging, or that could also double as your theme:

Fast-paced, otherworldly, and uplifting stories

Uplifting stories that get you thinking about otherworldly things
Optimistic trips with otherworldly companions

A little rough, but we're starting to get the hang of it. Let's try once more. Let's say your three words are:

1. Exciting
2. Escape
3. Love

The sentence might read:

I write exciting stories about love that help people escape.

That one made sense right away, so no need to adjust it. Now to brainstorm some potential taglines/short themes:

Escape to where love is exciting
Get away on a loving adventure
Where love always feels like an exciting escape

You could see one of these as a tagline under an author's name, right? The only problem is these are a little general, and they could apply to just about any author. How could you make your tagline more personal?

Creating That Personal Edge in Your Theme

To make your theme more personal, you'll need to focus specifically on your content. Your goal in the next exercise is to think about what themes recur in your stories or nonfiction pieces. Usually an author doesn't purposely write about a theme, but subconsciously it creeps into most every body of work he or she creates. It can be hard to narrow down, but here are some examples.

First, think about your protagonists. Do you create mostly troubled young women, lost older men, cowboys, cops, aliens, people who don't fit into the crowd or who have superpowers, vampires, doctors, rich women, entitled men, struggling teens, people dealing with sexual identity issues, people with emotional problems, lonely women, business men, spies, outcasts … ?

1. My characters are mostly _____.

Next, think about your settings. Are they mostly domestic, exotic, urban, rural, coastal, mountainous, otherworldly, dark and frightening, foreign, business-like, historical … ?

2. My settings are mostly _____.

Now we can insert these two words into our previous author theme formula, like so:

> I write _____ (word 1) stories in (setting description) settings about _____ (word 2 + character description) that help people _____ (word 3).

So continuing with the previous examples, we now have the following rough draft of your author theme, with the new additions underlined:

- I write fast-paced stories in <u>exotic</u> settings about <u>troubled</u> otherworldly creatures, helping people feel optimistic about life.

- I write exciting stories in <u>domestic</u> settings about <u>senior women</u> in love, helping people find escape.

Your theme is getting more specific, right? Of course, it's also getting longer. So once you have these descriptive words inserted, use your writing skills to clarify and tighten the theme a bit. The following examples are written using a more traditional tagline formula (a tagline is a catch phrase or slogan used to sum up a brand):

- Exotic trips with weird characters that leave you smiling

- Page-turning tales of the otherworldly kind

- Where older women find sexy love at home

- Romantic escapes for sexy older women

If you write nonfiction, then you can choose descriptive words that reflect the topic(s) you most commonly address, along with your typical target audience. So your sentence may look something like this:

I write informative stories in <u>urban</u> settings about the <u>disadvantaged</u> to help people find a way out.

And the theme/tagline may be something like:

- Shining the light for those living in the dark

- True stories about heroes from the underground

You can continue to pull three words from your list, add in your descriptive words, and see what you come up with. The more you play with it, the more ideas will pop up. Don't restrict yourself. If you think of other words that describe you and the work you do well, feel free to use them. The idea is to get your brain moving in this creative direction so you can eventually come up with a theme that works perfectly for you and your writing business.

Your Author Theme #1

It's time to take this a step further. Based on your answers, your experimentation with the author theme formula, and what we've talked about so far in the book, take a stab at writing your author theme below.

What's your author theme?

_____

Try this theme on for size and see if it fits. If not, come back and try again.

Applying an Author Theme to an Author Platform

Now that you have this theme (remember, you can always change it later), it's time to brainstorm how to use it across your entire author platform to tie your branding together. Turn to a fresh page in your journal and start thinking about the changes you need to make.

To begin, consider each of the following and how to adjust them based on your new theme. You don't have to make any of these changes this instant. The point is to get you examining all the elements with an eye toward a unifying theme. How might the following elements fit in this later evolution of your author platform?

Pretend we're talking about an author named Tim who's chosen the theme of "page-turning tales of the otherworldly kind." Let's look at each element of Tim's platform and think about how he might apply that theme.

Author Logo

A logo can give Tim a clear, visual way to communicate what he provides his readers. He can either hire a graphic designer to create one based on his author theme, or he can go to one of the many logo-creating websites on the Internet and create his own. (He can find them by Googling "logo maker.") This logo can be used on everything—business cards, bookmarks, website, social media channels, etc. It will provide a visual unity to the platform.

Website

Tim's website currently uses pastel colors, a small font, and few images. The site has no theme or tagline at the top of the homepage under his name. The blog posts are few and far between and announce only the events Tim is involved with, like book signings and readings.

Tim needs to design a website theme with a more exotic look, perhaps bolder colors, a larger "extraterrestrial-type" font, and larger photos. The header also needs to include his tagline and logo with the overall tone of the site giving readers a sense of exciting, otherworldly adventures.

Tim also needs to start posting regularly on his blog about space travel, exotic adventures, and other explorations that fit his theme—perhaps trips he's taken in real life or fantasy adventures he's created in a short story series. He could even feature other adventurists on his blog as a fun way to connect with like-minded people who may ultimately inspire him to create new story lines and characters.

Social Media

The header on Tim's social media pages needs to change from its present pastel colors and small fonts to match the boldness of his newly designed website. He should be using his logo and tagline across all social media channels. Then his posts need to mirror his new blog—stories about exciting adventures and the different people who take them, and perhaps some adventurous fails or humorous happenings—whatever best fits his personality and theme.

Author Swag

Tim isn't done yet. Next he needs to critically examine his bookmarks, posters, business cards, and other print products he uses to advertise his author brand. Do these match his theme or do they also require updating? Mandatory on this makeover is that his theme (tagline) is on everything, that the colors match his bold new look, and that he has some sort of exciting image or saying on all of his materials.

Book Launches/Signings/Giveaways

When Tim is about ready to release his next book or other product offering, he needs to circle back to his theme when thinking about how to launch it. He can make any event tied to this product more fun if he gets creative with his theme.

Just imagine if he had exotic music playing during a launch party that sets the mood his stories convey, or if he created an original, energetic presentation about an otherworldly adventure. He could get friends to demonstrate or describe how they experienced first-hand something exciting featured in his book. If his character went whitewater rafting, for instance, he could do a presentation on that with photos and/or video. Or he could explain how he came up with the otherworldly settings in his book, perhaps taking his audience on a virtual tour through one of his exotic towns.

If Tim's stories are more of the alien variety, he could have a theme-inspired launch party and encourage the attendees to come in costume. He could also have a hunt for mysterious prizes the attendees would need a map to locate, or he could do a presentation on a planet mimicking the setting featured in one of his stories. He could apply similar fun and original ideas to his book giveaways. Instead of just giving away the book, he could also include blueprints for his spaceship, or even instructions for how to build one at home out of easily procured crafting materials. If doing an online book tour, he could stipulate that guest posts incorporate his theme—and that he's hitting on "page-turning" and "otherworldly" in his interview answers.

The more Tim utilizes his theme, the more possibilities he'll come up with to communicate to readers what kind of experience they'll have while reading his books. That in turn means he'll more likely attract readers who are ready to respond to his work.

Sideshows

I use this word as a catchall to describe the many other activities writers can engage in to attract readers. Some writers may run online courses, incorporate art or photography into their posts, teach at writing workshops and conferences, go around to schools talking to kids, run writing retreats, or even get involved in advocacy or do brick–and-mortar book tours. The options reach as far as your imagination can go.

Natalie Bright, a children's author from Texas that I featured on *Writing and Wellness*, writes stories about rescue horses, and she partners with the horse owners to actually transport the horses to libraries and schools to meet children. Now that's a great idea! Of course, she has her books available for sale while she's there, and she features every rescue horse on her blog. Her theme is consistent and integral to her platform.

Think about the sideshows that you already do and how you can tie them into your theme. How can you adjust or change them to make them more effective? Or perhaps you need to come up with fresh ideas for other sideshows.

Keep Working Until You Find One That Fits

Thinking about the options explored in the last section will cause one of two things to happen:

1. You'll get more and more excited about your theme.
2. You'll feel less and less like this theme fits you.

The point of this exercise is to make sure your theme fits all aspects of your platform—at least on paper—and that it works with your personality and creative vision. It's more important the theme feel right than to get too caught up in whether it's the "perfect" theme, because as you naturally grow and evolve as an author and creative artist, you may need to periodically adjust your theme. The important thing is you find a theme that naturally unifies all your writing-related projects.

If the theme you found using the suggestions in this chapter works for you for now, fantastic. If it doesn't, then go through the exercises again. You can also use the following exercises if you need more assistance. Apply the same method as you did earlier—answer the questions, then put your "why" answers together to start digging for your theme.

Once you settle on a theme you feel good about, start making the relevant changes to your platform. You don't have to make them all at once—I find a gradual approach is best. The point is that you have the vision and the focus to start moving your marketing and outreach efforts into a more cohesive package. That way, your readers will understand exactly what you are offering when they land on your online doorstep or meet you in person. With consistency, this approach will help you build that audience you want.

1. Name three of your favorite memories, and explain why each memory meant so much to you.

2. Name three of your favorite paintings, and explain why each one is special.

3. If you could have your dream car, what make and model would it be? Why would this car be "the one"?

4. What animal best represents your creative nature? Why?

5. If you're a collector, name what you collect and why you like collecting that particular item. What does it represent for you?

6. Name two of your favorite television shows and explain why each show keeps you watching.

7. Name your favorite place—either somewhere you've been or somewhere you fantasize about visiting. This place inspires you and makes your imagination come to life. Describe where this place is, what it looks like, and why it's special to you.

Discover More: Using Your "Writing Strengths" List to Look for Themes

Throughout this book you've been keeping a record of your strengths in a master document. It's now time to make that list work for you as far as theme is concerned.

Simply copy and paste all the comments or reviews into one file, then as you did with your answers above, consolidate each comment into one or two words. I suggest making a table similar to this:

Name/Title	Comment	Themes
Betty (editor)	"you give such rich, lovely descriptions…"	Rich prose Good descriptions
John (reader)	"couldn't put it down"	Fast-paced
Carla (agent)	"many layers to this novel…"	Deep

The purpose of this table is to help you see themes emerge about the work itself. Breaking down what readers like about it or what they respond to helps you see the essence of what it is you do that inspires readers. Keep updating this document throughout your writing career, and it will continue to give you unique insights into your personal growth as a writer.

As you add comments to this table, ask yourself the following questions to understand more about what kind of writer you are.

1. What do people like about your writing? What words do they use when they're offering positive feedback? Examine the words and distill their meaning for a unifying theme.
2. What is the most common comment people make? Does it point to a theme, or is it something you should add to your theme?

CHAPTER 12
YOUR AUTHOR-
BUSINESS BLUEPRINT

Any time you launch a business, you include a mission statement that defines your purpose, goals, and values. It makes sense, then, that you'd have a mission statement for your author business. Why? Because a) you're in business for yourself, so you should operate like a business, complete with mission statement, and b) because it can help you to focus on those areas of your business that matter most.

Particularly when times get tough, or when you're inundated with choices and aren't sure which ones to pick, a mission statement can remind you why you're writing and what you ultimately want to accomplish. While a theme is about the reader or consumer and consists of one statement or phrase that reflects the essence of your work, a mission statement is more about you and what you mean to accomplish with your work.

As you go along in your career, it's easy to get sidetracked. You can become involved in so many activities that before too long, you may feel confused about which ones are most important. A mission statement can help you stay clear about your priorities, while making sure you're continuing to pursue only those goals that will take you toward the future you envisioned.

What Is a Mission Statement?

If you look up the term *mission statement* in the business dictionary, you'll find the following definition: "A written declaration of an organization's core purpose and focus that normally remains unchanged over time. Properly crafted mission statements (1) serve as filters to separate what is important from what is not, (2) clearly state which markets will be served and how, and (3) communicate a sense of intended direction to the entire organization."

These guidelines also work perfectly for a writer's mission statement. You need your mission statement to make clear what's important to you (and what's not), to clearly state your ideal reader and customer, and to communicate where you're going. It's like your true north, your ultimate guide, and the one thing you'll return to again and again when considering which choices you should make to move your career forward.

I'm going to help you create your own author mission statement, but first, a couple general rules to keep in mind: The statement should be in the present tense, so use phrases like "I do this" rather than "I did this" or "I will do this."

Next, keep the statement brief, usually no more than one paragraph. If you get too many thoughts tumbling on top of one another, it will be more confusing than helpful. If you get too wordy with your first few attempts, that's okay. You can edit it down later so you have a concise, clear statement that will serve you for years to come.

Creating an Author Mission Statement

To create your own mission statement, answer each of the following four questions with one sentence. Later you'll put these four sentences together to create the first rough draft of your mission statement, but try not to think too far ahead. For now, just focus on creating a one-sentence answer for each.

1. What do you do?

Your first answer may be "I write" or "I'm a writer," but we need to go beyond that. You want to get specific and creative with your answers. You can go back and use some of the notes you took when working on your author theme/tagline if you'd like. Think of it in terms of what you do as a writer that is *unique*. What's special about your writing and creative projects? What do you do that sets you apart?

If you're struggling, use this formula:

I _____ (action word or phrase) _____ (descriptive word) _____ (noun).

So for example:

I bring to life (action phrase) alien (descriptive word) worlds (noun).

I explore (action word) unusual (descriptive word) cultures (noun).

I reveal rarely-known historical figures.

I give voice to the unseen outcasts.

Okay, give it a try. It doesn't have to be perfect the first time. Just take a stab at it now and know you can always rework it later.

2. How do you do it?

Here's where you get more specific about the types of activities you want to incorporate into your writing business. This is all about your unique creative projects. So do you blog, write books, provide videos, teach courses, ghostwrite, edit, write for magazines, do research writing, provide grant writing services … ?

Write a simple sentence that tells how you do what you do. Here are a few examples:

I write short stories and books, and I have a robust informational blog.

I ghostwrite for a wide variety of clients, including business people and independent entrepreneurs.

I write books, teach workshops, and work in the schools to help kids find the joy in writing.

3. Who do you do it for?

This is where you identify your ideal reader and/or customer. Think of those people who really like your writing and the other creative projects you do. Who are those people? What characteristics do they share? If you haven't published yet, and you're not sure, imagine what they might be like.

Don't worry about age and gender. Go deeper. Are they people who want to experience other perspectives on life and love? People who want to escape to other worlds? People who want to imagine the exciting life of an international spy? People who wish to dive deeper into the nuances of unconventional relationships? People who are curious about their fears and want to experience them in a safe environment?

You don't even need to write a complete sentence for this one. Simply describe your reader/customer with a few words. For example:

Curious and future oriented

Members of unconventional families

Those interested in the world of spies

Sci-fi buffs who love aliens and UFOs

Women hooked on fiery romances

4. What value do you bring?

Focus on what your reader and/or customer gets out of interacting with you, your stories and books, and your other products. What does the reader take away from that experience? If you're not sure yet, what do you *want* them to take away? How do you want them to feel after they read one of your books or blog posts, or after they take one of your courses? Here are some examples:

They would gain a deeper understanding of certain modern-day issues (be specific about which issues)

They would feel uplifted with renewed hope for their lives

They would enjoy a safe form of entertainment they could return to again and again

They would thrill to an exciting ride that would leave them feeling invigorated

They would be encouraged to think more deeply about the big questions in life

Now that you have your four sentences (and partial sentences) down, weave them together into paragraph form. They probably won't flow well at first, so feel free to edit as necessary so the four sentences read as a cohesive paragraph. I'll give you some examples in the next section, but for now, just get something down you can work with.

Examples of Author Mission Statements

If your mission statement doesn't sound perfect yet—or even close— that's okay. I've included some examples that may help. Read these over, then recast your own mission statement, or simply set it aside and try again by creating fresh answers to the four questions.

Example 1

John A. Writer helps his readers experience exciting and thrilling adventures while stimulating their imaginations about what other life may exist beyond the realms of our understanding. Through his science fiction novels, online courses, and graphic art pieces, he shares his knowledge of otherworldly topics of interest, including UFO sightings, spacecraft designs, and possibilities for alien life, providing those who are future oriented with lots of exciting adventures to look forward to.

Looking at this example, you can see how we answered each of the four questions:

1. **What does John do?** He helps his readers experience thrilling adventures that stimulate their imaginations about unfamiliar types of life.

2. **How does he do it?** Through his novels, online courses, and graphic art pieces.

3. **Who does he do it for?** The future-oriented reader and customer who's interested in exciting new ideas about technology and space.

4. **What value does he bring?** He provides escape, adventure, excitement, and new ideas to think about.

Example 2:

Jill Ann Author helps readers feel at home. Through her novels, blog, motivational speaking, and family home-improvement projects, she inspires acceptance and understanding of various connections and relationships, uplifting those who seek unity in a conflicted world.

Looking at this example, you can see how we answered each of the four questions:

1. **What does Jill do?** She helps all types of families to build the homes they long for.

2. **How does she do it?** Through her novels, blog, and home-improvement projects.

3. **Who does she do it for?** Members of unconventional families or those seeking connection.

4. **What value does she bring?** She uplifts her readers; she provides hope that they can build the togetherness they're seeking.

Example 3:

Betsy B. Author challenges her readers to solve mysteries involving crimes against the disadvantaged. Through her novels, blog, and murder-mystery party plans, she brings to light the plight of the poor, downtrodden, and discriminated against, providing a satisfying sense of justice in a world where so often, justice is absent. Challenging her fans to put on their problem-solving hats, she presents intriguing puzzles that stimulate analytical minds, ending in solutions sure to satisfy.

See how Betsy answered each of the four questions:

1. **What does Betsy do?** She challenges her readers to solve mysteries while bringing to light the modern-day plight of poor and disadvantaged characters.

2. **How does she do it?** Through her novels, blog, and murder-mystery party plans.

3. **Who does she do it for?** Readers who care about helping the less fortunate and who enjoy the satisfaction that comes with solving a mystery.

4. **What value does she bring?** She allows readers to immerse themselves in problems that are eventually solved, giving them a sense of justice and completion that may be missing in their regular lives.

Okay, your turn. Look at your mission statement again, and adjust it with any changes you think necessary. Write your updated mission statement in your journal.

Putting it All Together: Your Author-Business Blueprint

Your author mission statement is now complete and can be added to everything else you've done so far in this book to create your author-business blueprint. This blueprint is a single document that holds all the crucial information you'll need to increase your chances of getting noticed. You'll use it as your personal compass to help you remember who you are, what you stand for, what you create, and what value you bring others.

Start by looking back over your answers throughout the book so far and use those answers to create a document or a table like the one here. If you can't fill out all the sections yet or you're not sure you want to keep what you have, that's okay. Just get something down for now. Remember, a lot of what you're going to do as an author entrepreneur also involves experimentation. So give it your best shot. Decide on something, and then try it out. You may want to create this blueprint in a new document on your computer to store along with your "strengths" table to make it easier to refer to later on.

Author Name (your name)

_____

Author Motivators (from chapter 4 quiz)

1. _____
2. _____

Author Strengths (top 3, from chapters 5, 6, and 7)

1. _____
2. _____

3. _____

Author Top 2 Cognitive Processes (from chapter 8)
1. _____
2. _____

Author Contribution (from chapter 10)

_____

Author Logo (if you don't have one yet, describe what it might look like)

_____

_____

Author Theme/Tagline (from chapter 11)

_____

_____

Author Mission Statement

_____

_____

_____

_____

And just like that, you've completed Part II of the book. Congratulations! You've now got a clearer picture of your writing business, so it's time to start putting what you've learned into action. Strap on your seat belt, and let's get this business of yours moving!

PART III:
PUSH YOUR BUSINESS FORWARD

*"Do you want to know who you are? Don't ask. Act!
Action will delineate and define you."*

~THOMAS JEFFERSON

CHAPTER 13

TAKE ACTION NOW

I'M ASSUMING YOU'RE feeling more confident about your future writing career and author platform. You've got a better idea about how to attract more readers and customers to your work, along with a good plan for how to better present yourself online so people understand clearly what sort of artist you are. What's next?

Don't lose momentum! If you're like most writers, you wait. You think, *Okay, that sounds kind of cool, let me think about it.* Don't! Saying to yourself, "I'll think about it" is dangerous to your career. You may not think so. After all, what could be wrong with waiting a bit to consider your next steps? Isn't that wise before taking action?

Absolutely not.

Three Reasons to Act Immediately!

1. Waiting feeds fear, action feeds confidence.

2. Waiting increases the risk of never doing anything at all.

3. Waiting makes you doubt yourself.

You've done the exercises, and now it's time to take action toward achieving your new goals ... at your *earliest opportunity*. I'm talking today, if possible, and if not, then tomorrow *at the latest*. It doesn't have to be a huge or time-consuming action. Even a baby step is better than nothing. This momentum can't be derailed if you want to increase your confidence and trust in yourself, which is vital for charting your own creative path to success.

1. Waiting Feeds Fear, Action Feeds Confidence

I've interviewed over 250 writers on *Writing and Wellness* and nearly all of them talk about having to deal with self-doubt somewhere along the way, usually more than once.

"I become plagued with self-doubt," says women's fiction writer Linda K. Sienkiewicz. "I fear I'm wasting my time, kidding myself when I say I'm a writer, flogging a dead horse." Linda overcame her self-doubt and went on to write the award-winning novel *In the Context of Love*.

But self-doubt isn't something you necessarily "get over" once you experience success. *USA Today* bestselling author Jennifer Bernard writes, "I wage a constant battle with self-doubt. I often think of it as an iron ball chained to my leg, slowing me down. It makes everything more difficult. Promotion is harder, bouncing back from rejection is harder. I wonder what the writing life would be like without it?" Jennifer has published many books, with her latest release (at the time of this writing) entitled *Hot and Bothered* (Jupiter Point Book 7).

Self-doubt can sabotage your progress in a number of ways. I referred to it as a "snake" in my previous book, *Overwhelmed Writer Rescue*, because of how it can slither in and out of your consciousness at just the right time to mess you up. It can create writer's block, cause you to abandon projects when they get tough, and even keep others from taking you seriously. Self-doubt's most devious tricks are:

- Causing you to doubt your instincts

- Stopping you from trying new things

- Keeping you from taking action

In chapter six we talked about how imposter syndrome, which is a close cousin to self-doubt, makes it difficult for you to trust in yourself and build confidence. Self-doubt works in a similar way. If you're trying to create your own unique writing career, it will likely try to sabotage you from the beginning, because it's going to make you question what your instincts are telling you, and what you've established so far in this book.

Self-doubt also tricks you into avoiding anything out of your comfort zone. You have to be brave to put yourself out there and risk making a mistake, but self-doubt will ensure you remember all the fears you have. The writing industry changes regularly and quickly. You have to be willing to rethink how you're doing things on a frequent basis if you want to keep your writing relevant and your marketing effective. When you want to try something new, however, self-doubt will do its best to convince you you're "not ready yet," or that you don't *really* need to try something else because what you're doing now is fine, or that you don't have the skills for this new project.

In the end, if self-doubt wins, the worst possible outcome occurs: inaction. You wait until you get smarter, have more time, feel stronger, or have a chance to think it over. Wait wait wait. What happens while you're waiting? Let's look at an example.

Women's fiction writer Lisa M. had self-published two novels and had experienced a moderate level of success. Both books were recognized in literary contests and both were selling at a steady trickle each month. Lisa was getting ready to release her third novel and wanted to step it up. In the back of her mind she heard this whisper: "Start a podcast!"

She had thought about it before. She loved talking to people and learning from them one-on-one. She believed one of her strengths was highlighting the strengths of others. But when the idea occurred to her, her first thought was, *No, I don't know how to do all that. I'd have to figure out how to record it and how to get it up on my website, and what about audio quality? I'd be clueless. And I'd probably have to invest in a microphone or something, and I just don't have time to get into it all.*

By the way, if you didn't recognize it, that's self-doubt talking. Lisa just had a great idea of what she could do to expand her reach, potentially make more connections, and sell more books, but right after she got the idea, she knocked it down. Let's say she keeps thinking about it, though. The next day, she imagines a person she might invite to appear on her new podcast. But then her self-doubt steps in: *Well, she's very busy. She probably wouldn't have time for me. I don't think I'd better ask her. Besides, I don't know what I'm doing. I don't want to embarrass myself.*

The next day, Lisa's podcast is more like a passing thought than a pressing one. The day after that, though the thought is still present, it's losing steam, and a week later, whenever Lisa thinks about the podcast, her mental response is, "Maybe later."

Then the death bell tolls. Lisa will release her new book the same way she released her former two books and *nothing will change.* All because she did one thing: she waited. And while she waited, her self-doubt worked overtime until it convinced her the idea was a bad one.

Dale Carnegie said, "Inaction breeds doubt and fear. Action breeds confidence and courage. If you want to conquer fear, do not sit at home and think about it. Go out and get busy."

Truer words were never spoken for writers. We are thinkers, obviously. We plot entire novels in our heads. We're not usually the types to do something on impulse, at least not something writing related. But if you want to blaze your own path here, which you need to do if you want long-term writing success, you can't afford to "think about" an idea. You need to act on it, *now*.

The action need not be large. In fact, I encourage you to make it small. In Lisa's example, she could have taken twenty minutes that night to research the idea or look for online courses about podcasting she might be interested in signing up for. Any action will do, because the point here is not to tackle the new idea in a day. The point is to *gauge your excitement*.

Once you take action on a new idea, you'll notice a change inside. You'll feel more energy and experience a more hopeful attitude about the future. Action creates enthusiasm, and as you take more action, that motivates you to take even more. It's a snowball effect, and all you have to do is get it started.

It's really cool when you experience it. I encourage you to try it at your earliest convenience. At this point in the book, you surely have some ideas of changes you want to make in your career. Think about just one. Perhaps you want to create a new logo, update your website, offer some new services, or invest in some sort of education. Whatever it is, if you take even a small action, you're much more likely to bring that idea to fruition, because small actions lead to other small actions, and that breeds *confidence*.

The surest way to believe you can do something is to do it—then next time, you'll feel more confident about it. It's easier than you think. The smallest action works. Try it!

2. Waiting Increases the Risk of Never Doing Anything at All

Waiting takes the wind out of your sails. You know how it is when you think of a new idea. You bounce around on your toes, imagining this new venture, but whoops, you have to go to work. You think maybe you'll look into it on your lunch hour, but then the boss calls you in for a meeting. After work, then, but the teacher calls and your son is sick. You go pick him up and think "after dinner," but you end up soothing your ill son until he finally falls asleep, and by that time, you're dead on your feet. You'll do it tomorrow, you think, but I caution you—that's a bad idea.

It's amazing how much juice just one day can sap from your enthusiasm. The next day that idea may seem even less possible, simply because of everything else that's going on in your life. You're more likely to get up the next morning and start thinking about all the reasons why it *won't* work. Your logical, analytical brain takes over and lists all the things you're already doing that won't leave time for anything new. That opens the door for your self-doubt snake to slither in and scare away your good ideas.

Waiting even one day makes it much less likely you'll ever do this new thing you thought of, and that's a shame, as that one slip can create a domino effect that takes you off your path. Not only does that deprive you of the step forward you might have taken in your career, it does something else even more dangerous: it threatens to create more distrust between you and your instincts.

3. Waiting Makes You Doubt Yourself

What you pay attention to grows and what you ignore shrinks. It's not enough just to come up with cool ideas. You must follow through and act on those ideas or risk losing trust in yourself.

Imagine if you were in a horrible accident and, as a result of your injuries, you went blind. You'd have to learn how to use your other senses to compensate, right? At first, you'd find that terribly difficult. You'd probably stumble and fall. You'd struggle to do everyday things that came easily before and might be tempted to stay in the house and hide away from the world.

But if you overcame your fear and went out anyway, gradually your hearing, your sense of smell and touch, and your "sixth sense" would take over. Eventually, you'd develop a whole new way of navigating the world, but only if you were willing to face the fear and allow yourself to develop those other senses.

Learning to trust yourself and your ideas as a writer is similar in many ways. You have to face the fear that maybe your ideas won't work out. You have to try new things, and perhaps stumble and fall. If you keep at it, though, you'll get better at running your business. You'll become more confident and feel stronger about accepting your own counsel. Soon, it will be like having your own career coach looking back at you in the mirror.

Ten Ways to Take Immediate Action

Here are examples of small actions that once you take them, can snowball into larger actions that eventually lead to success.

1. **Write a paragraph:** If your idea was about a new book, write a paragraph about it. Let the idea flow from your imagina-

tion to your hands, and get it down either on paper or in your computer. Don't be picky about it. Just get something down that you can look at and build upon the next day.

2. **Talk it out:** If you're on the go and can't stop to write it down, use your phone's voice capabilities to talk out an email or text message and send it to yourself. Or bring up your calendar and make a date with yourself to dig into the idea further.

3. **Research:** Get online and research your idea. Don't allow yourself to be sidetracked by other sites. Focus on the task you want to try and find out how you could do it. Take notes if you like.

4. **Write an outline:** If you're just bursting with an idea, take ten minutes and jot down an outline. I have had great luck doing this. I created the first outline for this book, for example, in one focused period of about an hour. Sometimes when an idea comes to you, it's fully formed and all you have to do is get it down.

5. **Tell a friend:** Nothing keeps us accountable like other people. If you have a good friend who's supportive of your writing, send a quick text that says, "Hey, I've got a great idea. Make me tell you about it tomorrow." That friend will likely follow through, which will force you to take additional action, even if it's only to get together with your friend to talk about it. (Always make sure you send ideas only to supportive friends. You don't need anyone raining on your parade at this point.)

6. **Put it on your to-do list:** If you're someone who's devoted to your list and who regularly takes action to cross items off, your new idea will bug you until you take action on it. So get

it on there and let the irritation begin! If you're someone who puts something on the list and then forgets about it, though, this step isn't for you.

7. **Print it out:** This is about creating a visual reminder. If you're short on time, print out a web page or image that represents someone who is already doing what you're thinking about doing. In Lisa's case, it would be the home page of a writer who's already running a podcast. She could print out the page that shows the picture of the writer, the name of the podcast, and some of the podcast topics. She could then tape this up near her writing space as a reminder that she needs to look into this.

8. **Send yourself a voicemail:** If you're an auditory person— you're partial to music and the sound of a loved one's voice—this could be a good way to take action on your ideas. Simply call and leave yourself a voicemail. Describe your new idea and talk about only the positive aspects of it, and how it might work to benefit you and your career. Then listen to it as soon as you can. This is also fun because you can replay the message down the road when you need a bit of encouragement.

9. **Clear your writing desk:** If you have had a really long day and you are about to drop, simply clear off your writing desk, tear off one big sheet of paper, and write on it in big letters, "Take action on [name idea] now!" Leave it in the center of your writing space (or somewhere else you'll be sure not to miss it), and take action on it the next day.

10. **Make yourself a promise:** Finally, if you simply cannot take any of these or similar actions, promise yourself you'll take action the next day, no matter what. Reserve any judgment on your idea until you do. It's vital to your career that you not allow your logical mind or your self-doubt to step in and interfere until you've taken at least some sort of action. Make that promise and keep it!

Remember, It's about Creating a Lasting Career for Yourself

You may ask yourself, "Why is it so vital that I take action on my ideas? I'm just trying to write a book and become a published author. So what if an idea or two passes me by? I'll still be working toward that goal."

Let me remind you what this is all about—creating a lasting writing career for yourself. That means it's important to take steps forward that will help you find your niche and establish a strong base from which you can continue to create. Persisting in doing only what you're already doing is unlikely to help you achieve that goal. Instead, listen to yourself, open your mind to new opportunities, and establish a true purpose behind what you're doing. The more you can do that, the more you'll secure your footing along this new path you're creating.

Discover More: Take Action on an Idea Now

Surely you have an idea right now for how to update, improve, expand, change, or adjust your writing business. Write it down in your journal.

My new idea is: _____.

Then write down the actions you will take right away—at least three.

This week, I will take the following actions on this idea:

1.

2.

3.

Now congratulate yourself, and keep going! Good luck.

CHAPTER 14

THE THREE BRAIN DECISION-MAKING SYSTEM

W HEN IT COMES time to actually make a decision to take action in your writing career, you may find that, on occasion, you get stuck. Should you really invest money in that writing conference, or save it to self-publish your book instead? Should you cut back on your hours at work so you have more time to devote to your business, or should you hire someone to help?

Making decisions can be frightening as we're never certain how they'll turn out. This chapter will give you a new tool to use that will increase the odds that your decision will be the right one for you and your career.

We'll start with a short quiz. I will be giving you minimal information as I want you to answer the questions as honestly as you can without preparation. Choose your answer based on what you do most of the time, then I'll fill you in on more later.

1. You have a definite opinion on a subject. Do you like explaining your reasoning to people?
   a. Yes. I can make charts, graphs, and demonstrate all the angles.
   b. Only to my closest friends.
   c. I'd have trouble putting it into words.

2. If you're offered a new job, what *most* influences your decision to accept or not?
   a. The salary, opportunity for advancement, and benefits.
   b. How attached I am to my current job/location and whether or not I will have friends at the new job.
   c. The vibes I picked up on during my interview.

3. You had an interesting dream that seems to relate to a decision you're about to make. You …
   a. Forget about it—dreams are just dreams.
   b. Definitely take it into account. Dreams are full of subconscious answers!
   c. Think it over; it may affect my decision depending on how I feel about it.

4. When you go on a blind date, do you make a snap decision about the other person?
   a. Yes, and usually it's right.
   b. Sometimes, if I get a strong feeling about the person.
   c. No, I reserve judgment until I get more information.

5. When considering a decision, do you make a list of pros and cons?
   a. Only if I'm extremely conflicted.

    b.   All the time!

    c.   If I do, it only frustrates me.

6.   You're meeting a friend at a coffee shop, and you get to choose. Which kind of place do you select?

    a.   One that has the best prices, the best selection, and is consistently reviewed as top notch.

    b.   One that offers a cozy, intimate place so my friend and I can really talk and enjoy one another's company.

    c.   One that has killer ambiance and great energy.

7.   It's election time. How do you choose your candidate?

    a.   I watch the candidates in action and choose the one who seems most confident and capable.

    b.   I research them all, then decide based on how their actions align on the issues.

    c.   I go for the candidate who champions the issues closest to my heart.

8.   Do you ever feel like you have a "sixth sense"?

    a.   Yes, often.

    b.   I've had moments that made me wonder, but I'm not sure.

    c.   I find that notion rather silly. Usually people use it to confirm what they already believe.

9.   If someone were to describe you with one word, which would you prefer?

    a.   Astute

    b.   Intuitive

    c.   Conscientious

10. Consider your past mistakes. Do you often think back on them?

    a. Yes, I continue to feel remorse, wondering what might have been.

    b. If I'm trying to learn something from them, yes, but otherwise, no.

    c. The past is the past. I prefer to live in the moment.

11. If you were to buy a lottery ticket, how would you choose your numbers?

    a. I'd let the machine choose randomly.

    b. I'd choose a sentimental date.

    c. I'd choose numbers that I have a good feeling about.

12. When you're making a difficult decision, you're most likely to experience…

    a. Racing thoughts and vertigo.

    b. A tug at my stomach.

    c. An ache in my chest, sometimes crying.

13. You're having a hard time making a decision. Why?

    a. I keep going back and forth because what's best for me might hurt someone else.

    b. I don't have a strong opinion either way yet.

    c. I don't have enough information yet.

14. You're browsing through an antique store when you find an item you *must* have. What is it?

    a. A cheap coin that I happen to know is incredibly valuable.

    b. A vintage toy that reminds me of a childhood memory or someone I cared about.

c. An item that just seems to "speak" to me through its energy.

Scoring: Now tally up your answers according to the guide below, adding up how many answers you have for each letter and letter combination.

1. a (H), b (HT), c (G)

2. a (H), b (HT), c (G)

3. a (H), b (G), c (HT)

4. a (G), b (HT), c (H)

5. a (HT), b (H), c (G)

6. a (H), b (HT), c (G)

7. a (G), b (H), c (HT)

8. a (G), b (HT), c (H)

9. a (H), b (G), c (HT)

10. a (HT), b (G), c (H)

11. a (H), b (HT), c (G)

12. a (H), b (G), c (HT)

13. a (HT), b (G), c (H)

14. a (H), b (HT), c (G)

Add up your numbers for each:

_____ G_____ HT_____ H

Now that you have your totals, let's talk about what your results mean.

We All Have More than One "Brain"

Neuroscience has discovered something fascinating over the past several years: we have complex and functional neural networks—or "brains"—in the heart and gut as well as the head. We used to think the brain was running the whole show, telling everything else in the body what to do, but recent research has found that's not always true. In fact, many times the communication starts in the heart or the gut, which then tells the brain what's going on.

In a 2011 study, scientists conducted an experiment in which they hooked up participants to an electroencephalogram (EEG), then showed them various images, some neutral and some emotionally affecting. They found the heart rate changed *in anticipation* of seeing the emotional images. In other words, the heart responded to those images before the person saw them *and* responded even before the brain did.

The researchers wrote, "surprisingly, the heart appears to receive and respond to intuitive information." They also found that females were more in tune to these intuitive communications than males were.

Turns out the heart has its own intrinsic nervous system and neurons (messengers) just like the brain, and it can take in information, process it, and communicate it to the brain (rather than the other way around). Studies have found that, in some ways, the heart seems to have its own logic—not always just following orders, but going its own direction, acting independently, and sending messages to the brain that the brain then obeys. In a way, it's like a second brain.

The gut has similar qualities. It also contains neural tissue and neurons—more than are found in the spinal cord or peripheral nervous system. In fact, embedded in the lining of the gastrointestinal tract is what scientists now call the "enteric nervous system (ENS)," similar to the central nervous system. It is a network of neurons, neurotransmitters, and proteins that sends messages back and forth as well as to the brain. Also called the "second brain" because of its size and complexity, the gut has been found in studies to be involved not only in digestion and overall health, but also in emotions, mood, and decisions.

Scientists from Florida State University reported in 2017 that gut-to-brain signals have a powerful influence on us. They found in their research that the "gut feelings" we get are real messages from the ENS and can stop us from making mistakes. Interestingly, they also found our diet can have a major impact on the quality of these signals—whether they're "wise" or not. A high-fat diet, for example, can lead to inflammation in the gut, which can change the messages it's sending from happy and energetic to depressed and anxious.

We also have trillions of bacteria in the gut that make up what's called the gut microbiome. A healthy gut has a good balance of good and bad bacteria, but if the bad start outnumbering the good, we can experience not only physical problems, but emotional ones too. Studies have shown this delicate balance may be implicated in a variety of stress-related conditions, including anxiety and depression.

All of this research has led to a new field of leadership development called "multiple brain integration techniques (mBIT)." According to Suzanne Henwood and Grant Soosalu, who presented a paper on the subject at the International Leadership Association (ILA) 16th Global Leadership Summit, this decision-making system "provides leaders with practical methods for aligning and integrating their three brains for increased levels of emergent wisdom in their decision-making…"

In a nutshell, Henwood and Soosalu recommend incorporating all three "brains" when making decisions, with the idea that doing so will result in a wiser decision-making process that provides increased benefits to everyone involved.

People being people, however, we have our strengths and weakness, and it's no different when we're talking about the three "brains." We all tend to favor one of them over the other two. That's what the quiz was about. Let's find out what your answers meant.

Finding Your Dominant Decision-Making Brain

Look back at the end of the quiz, and using the numbers you recorded for each of the three areas, find out which one is your dominant brain. Then read more about this brain and how it works.

1. The Head (H)

If you had the highest number of points in the "H" category, you prefer to make decisions with your head. You're mostly interested in gathering the facts, weighing the pros and cons, and figuring things out logically. You try not to let your emotions interfere too much, as you believe they can just get in the way of deciding what's right or what's best. You may make spreadsheets or charts to help you compare the potential outcomes of each decision you're considering.

How it feels: When thinking about an issue, you may:

- feel like your thoughts are racing
- feel light-headed

- get a headache

- feel tension in the back or front of your head

Strengths: Sense of logic, analytical ability, adherence to the facts. You do your research and come to the table prepared and knowledgeable.

When writing: You feel particularly proud when someone says your writing is clever or intelligent.

Drawbacks: Some may say you overthink things. You can get stuck in analysis paralysis, forever going over the facts, the numbers, and the other things you must consider in your attempt to make the right decision. This can delay you in deciding at all, which can negatively affect your career. You can also get so caught up in making the "right" or "best" decision you neglect other considerations that also matter, like your feelings (or others' feelings), your health, or your creative well-being.

2. The Heart (HT)

If you had the highest number of points in the HT category, you make most of your decisions with your heart. Your feelings and emotions rule, and you put a high priority on your values and your connections with others. You focus on what's important to you in life and experience an emotional link to your dreams and aspirations. When making decisions, you always take into account those things you care about, what your desires are, and how the decision will affect your important relationships.

How it feels: When thinking about an issue, you may:

- feel a tightness in your chest

- have difficulty breathing

- feel a "pull" at your heart

- feel a "swell" of emotion in your chest

Strengths: Deep feelings, concern for others, understanding the value of relationships. You know what you want and feel an emotional connection to your dreams and desires, but you always consider others too.

When writing: You feel particularly proud when someone says your book made them cry or filled them with joy.

Drawbacks: When you feel extreme emotions—either good or bad—they negatively affect your decision-making ability. Feeling sad or depressed can make you hesitate or refuse an opportunity, while feeling elated or super-energized can make you jump into a situation that might not be good for you. You may assume you know how others feel before they actually tell you. Your concern for others can sometimes lead you down the wrong road, particularly if you put your own needs last.

3. The Gut (G)

If you had the highest number of points in the "G" category, you prefer to make decisions with your gut. You are an intuitive person who finds it easy to tune in to energy, vibes, and unseen messages from the world around you. You get a "feeling" of what your decision should be, but you may have a hard time explaining your choice to others. Your decision power can be cryptic and secretive, or you may feel like you hear a "little voice" telling you which way to go.

How it feels: When considering an issue, you may:

- get a physical sensation of excitement or dread in your stomach

- feel your stomach "twist," "drop," or "lift"

- feel a tightness or sense of energy in the gut

- suffer from digestive issues like bloating or diarrhea

Strengths: Instincts, intuition, ability to make connections between seemingly unrelated items, experiences, or occurrences. You can step back and look at the whole picture and get flashes of insights that help you envision the future you want.

When writing: You feel particularly proud when someone "gets" what you were trying to say in your writing.

Drawbacks: At times, you may make quick, impulsive decisions without having all the information you need, neglecting the fact that you could discover new information tomorrow that might change your mind. Because you rely on your gut response, your personal biases may also get in the way at times. Also, you may have trouble trusting your insights—if you ignore your inner voice in favor of what appears to be a more logical approach, you could make the wrong decision for yourself.

What If You Had a Tie?

Sometimes, people end up with a tie between two of the dominant brains. If this happens to you, it may mean you use both equally well. Watch yourself more carefully over the next couple weeks to see which you may favor when making decisions, but it is possible you go back and forth between the two on a regular basis.

What Are Your Brains Saying to You?

Let's put what you've learned so far into practice. Set aside about ten minutes to go through the following exercise:

First, think about a decision you need to make right now. It's best if it involves your writing career. Maybe you're considering updating your website, offering new services to your clients, trying a new type of writing, going to a writing workshop, hiring an editor, signing a publishing contract, self-publishing, or setting up a book signing. Write down the decision you're considering in the form of a question. For example, "Should I spend the money to go to this conference?"

Should I: _____?

Now get comfortable (if you aren't already), close your eyes, and place your hand on your belly. Take in several deep breaths and center yourself so you can hear your inner voice. Feel the air on your skin and hear the sounds in the room. Imagine the sky above you and outer space beyond that. Prepare your pen or typing fingers to respond immediately—no waiting. Then ask yourself the question again. Focusing on any flashes of insight you receive, *immediately* write down your answer. Don't wait or analyze it. Just write.

My GUT says I should:_____.

Now place your hand on your heart. Take another couple deep breaths and close your eyes. Focus on the beating of your heart. Feel it pulsating under your fingers. Pay attention to how you *feel*, and what your desires are. Concentrate on feelings of love, and imagine a sense of peace and harmony. Then ask the question again and write down your answer:

My HEART says I should:_____.

Now place your hand on your forehead. Take another couple of deep breaths and close your eyes. Tune in to your thoughts. Imagine them speaking to you. Set your emotions aside and focus on what you *think*, and what makes sense logically and practically. Ask the question again and write down your answer:

My HEAD says I should:_____.

Now examine the three answers. Do they all agree? If so, great! You've got your decision. If you can get all three to align, that is the best outcome and the one most likely to get you the results you want.

If you've got one answer disagreeing with the other two, it's time to dig a little deeper. First, ask yourself if the disagreeing brain is your dominant one. Write your answer below:

Is my disagreeing brain my dominant one? _____ (Y/N)

If it is, pay close attention: **Never go against your dominant brain.** You will not be happy with the results. Even if the other two agree, if your dominant one is screaming the opposite message, you need to listen. Take the time to figure out why it's disagreeing and regroup before making a decision. In the end, if you can't get your dominant brain to agree, don't move forward.

If the disagreeing brain (or brains) is/are nondominant, however, that's a different situation. First, ask yourself: "Does my dominant brain agree with one other brain?"

_____ (Y/N)

If yes, you may still be able to move forward. If only one brain disagrees, and it's not your dominant, find out why that other brain doesn't agree.

My _____ (name of brain) disagrees because: _____

_____.

Examine that answer. Then assign it a weight of importance on a scale from 1–10.

This is how important to me? _____ (1–10)

If the level of importance is six or higher, give yourself more time to make the decision. See if you can satiate this disagreeing brain by adjusting the decision slightly or by putting some safeguards in place. If your heart and gut say you should go to the conference, for example—and you're a heart-dominant person—but your head is balking, ask yourself what the source of the disagreement might be. Maybe you're worried about finances. If that's the case, you can start saving now or decide to put in some extra hours at work to help earn the difference. That may be enough for your head to give you the green light.

If the level of importance is five or lower, however, you probably don't need to worry about what this disagreeing brain thinks. Most likely, you can move forward with your decision.

What if you have two other brains disagreeing with your dominant brain? Then you should probably wait and do some more thinking before you decide. If your gut and head say you should not go to the conference, and only your dominant heart wants to go, use the steps above to find out why these other two brains are disagreeing, and then assign a level of importance to each answer. Consider the reasons carefully and try to find ways to appease at least one of these other brains before moving forward.

Even though most of us prefer one mode of decision-making over the other two, each of us uses all three to some extent. Doing so purposefully can help give you more clarity in your decision-making process and can also help you not fall into the negative side of your strong suit.

Having all the facts in a situation (head) can help you avoid making an impulsive decision (gut) that would hurt you. Checking in with how you feel at the moment about your career (heart) can ensure that logic and analysis (head) don't kill your creativity or motivation. Taking a long walk to get calm and gain a sense of what decision you want to make (gut) can help your emotions (heart) not sway you the wrong way.

And though we used basic yes/no questions in the exercise, if you need more information before deciding, you can also ask all three brains open-ended questions. You may ask, "What is the next step I need to take to push my business forward?" Pose the question to each brain in turn and see what they each have to say. You may gain some insights that help you zero in on which activity you should tackle first.

Three's a charm. In most situations, try to get all three brains to agree. Two often works just fine, as long as one is your dominant. The important thing is to decide and move forward!

Four Ways to Increase Your Odds of Making a Good Decision

In addition to using the three-brain system, here are four suggestions to help you make the best possible decisions:

1. Give yourself time.

Rushed decisions often turn out badly because they ratchet up emotions and skew decision-making strengths. In a 2015 study, researchers asked participants to decide whether or not to take a risk. One group was told they had to make the decision quickly. The other group had unlimited time to do so. The researchers also manipulated the participants' emotions by having them view a happy, sad, or neutral movie clip.

Results showed those who were under a time crunch were far more likely to make risky decisions when they were feeling happy, and less likely to do so when they were feeling sad. But those who had plenty of time to decide were not affected by their emotions.

A risky decision could be a good one or a bad one for you—the point is if you're pressured to make that decision quickly, your emotions could negatively affect your decision. It's always best to give yourself plenty of time.

2. Give yourself a deadline.

Of course, give yourself *too much* time and you may avoid ever making a decision at all. In the end, that *is* a decision—a decision *not* to act, which is often the wrong decision for your writing career.

Here's where giving yourself a deadline can help. Choose an amount of time that is equal to the difficulty of the decision. If you're trying to decide between two publishing offers, that's a pretty big decision. If you're trying to decide whether or not you should go to a conference and you're financially strapped, that could also be a big decision. Give yourself a couple weeks. If you're trying to decide whether to do a guest post for a blog you admire, however, that's a smaller decision. Give yourself three days at most.

Some decisions require more time. If you're thinking about self-publishing, and you've never done it before, give yourself several weeks to really understand the effort, money, and time it will take to create a quality book. A month or so should work.

You get the idea. The deadline should conform to the importance or long-lasting effects of the decision, but create a deadline, and do your best to stick to it.

3. Get fear out of the equation.

If there's one thing that can stop you from taking that next important step, it's fear. Your gut, heart, and head may be telling you it's time to do X, but if you're afraid of that step, you'll find some reason not to.

Studies show when the fear part of the brain is turned on, any desire we may have to explore or take risks (of any kind) is turned off.

That can be bad for your future, as any step forward is always going to involve risk and exploring your options and possibilities is critical to finding new opportunities to pursue.

Other studies have found when fear influences us, we tend to focus only on the negative, and in particular, on possible catastrophes. Let's say you have an opportunity to participate in a public reading for the first time, but you're nervous about it. That fear can override your good decision-making skills and lead you to imagine not only failing, but totally humiliating yourself, to the point that you turn the opportunity down.

Fear can come in at any time in your writing career. You may fear change, judgment, failure, scarcity, the unknown, or a zillion other things. This fear can also manipulate you into believing you're using your dominant brain when you're really not. After all, you "feel" this fear, and it feels safer to avoid the risk, so you think you're making a heart-based or gut-based decision, when actually it's the fear deciding.

To make sure fear is not messing with you, first, ask yourself if you're afraid of something. Be honest. Journal about it. If you find fear is playing a role, imagine your decision, whatever it is, can only turn out well. Then what would you decide?

Next, ask yourself: "What can I do to avoid what I fear?" Write down possible solutions and see how they may sway your decision.

Finally, ask yourself, "Which decision would help me grow as a writer and an artist?" Then use your three brains to answer.

4. Realize that good decision-making is a skill.

Did you know people can suffer from "decidophobia?" It's an actual phobia that means "fear of making decisions." This is different from what we just finished talking about. You don't fear what may happen as a result of your decision, but instead, actually fear the act of making a decision. You're afraid you'll make the wrong one, so you do everything you can to skip it entirely. You may just go along with other people and let them decide or turn to an authority figure, psychic, or guru for answers.

Some people become so concerned about this they experience physical symptoms when faced with a decision, such as dry mouth, sweating, muscle tension, nausea, dizziness, or other symptoms of anxiety.

Decidophobia can be a serious mental illness that benefits from psychiatric treatment, but for many creative people, it exists in a milder form. Still, it can be just as debilitating to your career. After all, you have to make decisions when you're the captain of your own ship, right? You simply can't avoid it forever.

How can you get over this fear? Practice. One of the best ways is to use the methods described in this chapter to come to a decision, and then make it, even if you're scared. Try to focus on small decisions at first, such as when to write your query letter or what writer's conference to attend. The more you do it, the more your skills will grow and eventually it will feel less frightening.

It may also help to realize in most cases, you can recover from a bad decision. Most of the decisions we make aren't matters of life or death. Even if you choose to sign a contract with a publisher and it turns out to be a dud, it's not the end of the world. You can write another book and try again.

We have to make mistakes to learn. Realize that decision-making is something you will get better at as you go—and be willing to fail once in a while. You'll still be creative, you'll still be a writer, and you'll be able to make a better decision next time.

Experiment and Be Willing to Fail

Now that you've completed this chapter, you have a good handle on using the three-brain, decision-making system to make good decisions in your writing career. Hopefully you'll start making some right away and experiment to see how they turn out.

CHAPTER 15

TAKE THAT LEAP

MY FIRST JOB as a writer was for a large international corporation. It was the perfect start to the writing life, as I did every type of writing you can imagine. I started out as associate copywriter, writing magazine articles, speeches, interview-based articles, reports, and white papers, as well as copy for brochures, commercial scripts, convention displays, product identity, and catalogs, to name just a few.

Then I was promoted to senior writer and eventually to managing editor where I managed a team of writers and print production personnel, editing the writers' work and guiding them toward improvement while making sure all the projects got to print on time.

The salary was good, the promotions came quickly, and there were frequent bonuses. But then my boss left the company for another opportunity and things went downhill. For a while the finance guy oversaw our team, and since he was a numbers person and not a marketing person, all the copy became twice as long as it needed to be. Our poor graphic designers were struggling to fit book-length content onto a round shake mix container! (As if the customers would really read all that.)

They finally hired a new boss for our department, but within a few weeks, we knew we were in trouble as she was holding company meetings at her house while in her pajamas. I had been toying with the idea of doing something more flexible with my writing life for a while, but the arrival of our new pj-clad boss quickly moved up my timing. My intuition was telling me freelance was the way to go. I'd be able to set my own hours and thereby work on my novel-writing more intently. I loved the idea, but it was a big risk.

As a freelance writer, I would have no security. At the company, I had a full-time salary, bonuses, and benefits, including an IRA-match. The longer I was their company employee, the more money I would have earned, but I knew the corporate life wasn't for me long-term. I was grateful for what I had learned, but spending the rest of my life basically giving all my creative energy to the corporation wouldn't make my dreams come true.

I had to decide: suck it up and stay at the corporation—which was becoming increasingly difficult because of the poor leadership and insane hours—or take a giant risk and see if I could make it as a freelancer.

And so we come to the subject of this chapter—taking risks. As a writer wanting to get his/her work out into the world—and hopefully make some money while doing it—you are choosing to be an entrepreneur. Gone are the days when you could just hand your book over to a publisher and let them take care of "all that." Authors are now responsible for growing their own businesses, which may be difficult, but can also be exciting.

Are You a Risk Taker?

How do you feel about risks? Do you dive in or wait? Do you frequently act without knowing what the outcome might be, or are you more likely to hang back and think about it? Interestingly enough, your attitude is likely genetically programmed into you. In a 2009 study, researchers reported that individuals vary in their willingness to take financial risks, and the variations may be based on two specific genes. Those carrying one variation of the first gene were found to take 28 percent less risk than those carrying another variation, while those carrying one variation of the second gene took 25 percent more risk than those with a different variation.

Genetics can be complicated, but the point is your behavior regarding risks is likely in your DNA. Studies of classical twins estimated genetic effects accounted for about 20 percent variation in risk taking. Researchers have also discovered that neurotransmitters in the brain, like dopamine and serotonin, play important roles in decision-making and that genes may regulate the production of these neurotransmitters in such a way as to affect risk-taking behavior.

So whatever your viewpoint on taking risks, you're likely stuck with it. That doesn't mean, however, that you can't take risks in service to your writing career. I myself am not a risk taker in general. When I learned to ski (somewhat), I was cautious. I wasn't one of those skiers who charged down the hill hooting with glee. I like some risk—I learned to fly a plane and to ride a motorcycle—but these were both in lessons with a teacher. I wasn't grabbing my friend's bike and heading out into the hills on a dare. I'm generally careful with finances, and I don't like to be in debt.

But I took that leap and quit my corporate job to start a freelance writing career, and that choice has made all the difference.

Why Taking Risks Is Important to Your Writing Business

I worked with a lady once who wanted more than anything to quit her job and open a dessert shop. She talked about it at least a couple times every week. She made special desserts and brought them into the office. She mused over what her shop would be like. She scoured the paper for ads about building spaces she could rent. She complained almost daily that she was still in the same dead-end position. Yet over ten years later, she was still working in that same office and had done nothing to move herself any closer to her dream.

She was afraid to take the risk.

The thing is, wanting something, talking about it, dreaming about it, and even writing about it is not enough. Your motivation must be strong enough to overcome the obstacles in your way, and your commitment must be powerful enough that you're willing to take risks. But risks, by their very nature, are frightening. You may gain what you want ...

- fame

- book sales

- a book publishing contract

- more time to write

- money from freelance writing

... but you could also lose something that's important to you:

- money

- pride

- time

- status

It's unfortunate that most of the time, we get caught up thinking about what we could gain and worrying about what we could lose, because it means we're ignoring a third option: learning. Every time you take a risk, you learn more about yourself and your writing career. Even if it doesn't turn out the way you hoped, you still benefit from the experience. You learn you can take risks, which is likely to boost your confidence. And you learn what worked and what didn't, so you can take an even better risk the next time.

Why would you want to become better at taking risks? There are many reasons, most of which have to do with your creative career, but some that go beyond that. Risk takers, for example, may be smarter! Researchers reported in a 2009 study that participants who were more likely to take risks had more white matter in their brains than those who chose to play it safe. White matter contains the neural network—it is the communication hub where nerve impulses fire to transmit information from one section to another. Researchers theorized that the risk-taking participants probably sought out challenges that regularly stimulated their brains, promoting the growth and development of a robust neural network.

We also have some evidence that risk takers may be happier. One study of over twenty thousand people found that, in general, those who were more likely to take risks in life were more content and satisfied with their lives than those who avoided risks. The scientists admitted they weren't sure which came first. Were the satisfied people more optimistic and satisfied to begin with, and thus more likely to take risks? Or was it *because* they took risks that they ended up more satisfied with their lives? We don't know for sure, but we can imagine how someone may end up staying in an unhappy situation simply because they're unwilling to take a risk.

In that same study, researchers found something interesting— self-employed people were less cautious than those who worked for a company or a boss. We've been talking about how writers must run their own businesses here, so this makes sense. If you're a writer who's making a full-time living, you're working for yourself, and you'll be faced with many risky decisions over the course of your career. Even if you're only a part-time writer, you're still in business for yourself if you intend to sell magazine articles, books, courses, or other materials down the road. You're an entrepreneur, and entrepreneurs take risks when they need to.

Here's another finding: risk takers in general are more optimistic people. They're more willing to take chances because they believe things will work out well for them. They expect to win. They understand they may lose from time to time, but they don't worry about it too much because they know in the end they'll come out on top. Optimism is tied to a number of personal benefits as a whole, including better health and longer life, so that's another bonus for risk takers.

The greatest benefit to you, as a writer or creative artist seeking to build your own business, is the more risks you take along the way, the more you'll develop skills you need to sustain a successful career. These include:

- Overcoming fear of failure

- Being willing to make mistakes

- Learning what risks are worth it

- Building your business acumen

- Developing confidence in your decision-making skills

So whether or not you are a risk taker in general, you can become a smart risk taker in your writing business.

Risk-Management Solutions to Help You Take Smarter Risks

Let's say you're considering taking a risk. It could be a financial risk, like investing in new home-office equipment, a business risk like self-publishing a book, a creative risk like trying an entirely new type of writing, or an emotional risk like submitting your work to several agents, editors, or contests. As in the last chapter, you'll need a specific idea in mind to proceed with the following exercises. Whatever risk you're considering, write it down in your journal.

I'm considering taking the following risk for my writing business:

_____

I'll share with you a risk I took. I'd been operating a successful full-time freelance writing business out of my home for about seven years when my biggest client, who had been delivering the bulk of my income, suddenly disappeared. I was working then for Gerber Baby Products as the writer and editor for their quarterly magazine, *Pediatric Basics*. The magazine was distributed to about fifty thousand pediatricians every three months and provided Gerber with a great tool for marketing their products to doctors who were likely to recommend them to parents.

Then one day I heard from my team that Gerber had sold out to Nestlé, a foreign company, and the powers-that-be at the corporation didn't know if Nestlé would want to continue the magazine or not. The general consensus was that they would, as the magazine had a great reputation, but for months we just didn't know. We continued to work on the next issue, as usual, until around April of 2008, when much of the rest of the U.S. national market was struggling. That month, we were informed that Nestlé was pulling the magazine. It was done, and so were we.

That year proved to be one of the most difficult in my freelance career because I wasn't ready for that sort of change. Things had gone so well with Gerber that I had neglected my website and online presence, so when I found myself back in a position where I needed to hustle for new clients, I was woefully unprepared. By the fall of that year, finances had become extremely tight; it had gotten to the point I was going to have to either get a job (whatever position I could get quickly) or take out an unsecured loan to pay the bills for a few more months, in the hopes that I could use that time to breathe new life into my business.

I wanted to take the loan because I was afraid if I went out and got a job, that would be the end of my freelance career. At the same time, the idea of having yet another payment was equally frightening, as I had very little money coming in (from a few small clients I'd had on the side all along).

What to do?

What's the Worst That Could Happen?

Now that you have your risk in front of you, the first thing you're probably thinking about is everything that could go wrong. That's okay. Let's work with that for a minute. In fact, anytime you're considering a risk, this is a good first step to take: write down what may happen if this risk doesn't work out the way you hope it will. Might you:

- Experience a financial setback? (How long would you need to recover?)

- Spend a lot of time on something you can't use?

- Fail to create the project you wanted to create?

- Experience a blow to your self-confidence?

- Struggle to manage because of other things going on in your life right now? (Change of jobs, family demands, illness, etc.)

- Invest your time and money only to find it didn't help your business?

Let me go through and answer these possible scenarios using my example. I wanted to take the loan, but if I did, what could go wrong? Here's my list:

- Three months later, I could be in worse financial trouble than I already was.

- I could fail to find the clients I needed and still have to get a job. (This was the worst that could happen, in my opinion.)

- I could feel like I had failed big time—I'd had a thriving freelance business, and I'd lost it.

- I could be putting myself and my future more at risk by taking on another debt.

- I could lengthen the amount of time I'd have to spend worrying about income.

Your turn, now. Write down in your journal all the negative things you may experience if this risk doesn't go well. Don't forget to write down the worst that could happen.

If this risk doesn't turn out well, the following may occur:

Now that you've identified all the potential problems, it's time to put on your problem- solving hat.

Problem Solving: Can You Improve Your Odds?

You've listed the potential problems, and now it's time to tackle them one by one. How could you address these problems and increase the odds that things will go well for you?

Let me continue with my example, starting with the worst that could happen. When the loan ran out, I could have failed to find more clients and still have had to get a job. How to reduce the odds of that happening? Here's what I came up with:

- Update my website so it looks more attractive to potential clients (consider getting professional help).

- Update my résumé so it targets the type of clients I'm looking for (consider getting professional help to create the best résumé possible).

- Research freelance job websites and start checking them every day.

- Create a stronger cover letter and portfolio for pitching new clients.

- Start pitching magazines and other paying publications.

- Continue to live as frugally as possible.

The cool thing about this sort of problem solving is it forces you to open your eyes to the weaknesses in your business. As I examined what could go wrong and how to increase my odds of successfully rebuilding my clientele, I realized I had neglected my website, failed to update my portfolio with recent work, and lost track of current freelance job websites. These are all things I should have been maintaining all along, but because I was so comfortable working for Gerber, I hadn't looked ahead at the possibility that things could change.

I now know better! And that's another lesson the whole situation taught me—it's always best to be ready for the situation to change and to change quickly, and to have your business in a strong place where it can survive.

Your turn. Look at the list you created, and brainstorm what you can do to increase your odds that things will turn out perfectly. If one of those potential problems is financial, can you spend a few months saving up for this change? Can you cut back on expenses? Can you combine resources with someone else so you can get by on less? Can you sell some items to earn extra money, or take on some part-time work for a while?

If the problem was that you needed to develop more skills first, can you do that now? Can you take an online course, a writing workshop, or a marketing workshop that would help you feel more confident about taking this step? If you're thinking about changing jobs or cutting back on the one you have, can you go back to the original situation in a few months if you have to? Can you cut back temporarily? Can you get someone to step in and help for a limited time?

Whatever problems you listed, try to think of potential solutions and write them down in your journal.

What Will It Cost You Not to Take This Risk?

Now it's time to turn the tables and think about what will happen if you *don't* take this risk. Most of the time we focus all of our thoughts on what might go wrong if we *do* take the risk and ignore the real consequences of what could happen if we fail to take action.

Here's where you need to take stock not only of your writing career, but your creative self. Are you still motivated and energized? Do you wake up eager to get to work every day? Are you still excited about the future? Or are you getting tired, burned out, discouraged, or bored?

As creative people, we need to be moving forward, challenging ourselves, and seeing our progress if we are to stay in the game. If we go too long without experiencing these things, we can start to stagnate, slow down, and lose hope. You are the machine behind this career, which means your growth and development are critical to your success.

Will this change encourage your growth? Will it inspire you, energize you? Will it help you feel like you can make your dreams come true? If so, those are important benefits, and you want to be sure to give them the weight they deserve. Too often we focus only on the financial issues. You may think, for example, it's best to continue working at the job you have, even though you're bored and it's limiting the time you have to spend on your writing. Or you may think you have to stay in one particular genre because your publisher is happy with your success, even though you're bored and getting burned out writing book after book on an accelerated schedule.

Here's where you must put on your fortune-telling hat and look into the future. Where will you be a year from now? How about five years from now? If you keep going and *don't* make this change you're considering, how will you feel then?

It's also important to think about your health. If you're killing yourself working umpteen hours at a day job and then working all hours on your writing business, too, you will probably not be able to sustain that for long. You may already be feeling tired and irritable. If that's the case, it may be to your benefit to take the risk you're considering sooner rather than later, particularly if the change will help ease your schedule and give you more time to manage all your responsibilities.

Of course, you need to consider your family, too, and how the change may affect them. But before you jump to the conclusion that the risk would be too difficult, consider having a family meeting about it. Maybe some of the other family members would be willing to pitch in and help. Maybe your kids would rather see you home more often than working all the time, and would be willing to tighten their financial belts to make that happen. Maybe they'd also be willing to sacrifice some things to see you happy and pursuing your dreams.

What will it cost you not to take this risk? Consider this carefully before making your decision. Let me continue with my example. If I didn't take out the loan, what would it cost me?

- I could lose my freelance business entirely and be stuck working for someone else for who knows how long. (The worst that could happen.)

- I could end up in a dead-end job five years down the road.

- I could feel like my future had lost its promise.

- I could lose my inner sense of drive and ambition.

Your turn. What will it cost you not to take this risk?

_____

What's Plan C?

Let's say you've decided it isn't a good time for this change, or that the obstacles are too many right now. Before you abandon the idea completely, ask yourself if you have a plan C. Could you take a baby step forward? Could you shrink the risk somehow? Could you make a small change that will still get you closer to your goal, but doesn't present so many potential problems?

When you can't take big leaps forward, you must take little hops instead to get where you want to be. Sometimes you must also force yourself to consider an alternative course of action that may end up being your best possible career move.

Here's what happened to me. After I examined all the issues and problem solved as best I could, I decided to take out the loan. Then I started doing the things I needed to do to increase my odds of recruiting clients and getting my business off the ground again. Meanwhile, I was still concerned about money, so I considered a plan C: a part-time job. Could I somehow make money without having to devote the bulk of my time to an employer so I could retain the time I needed for my business?

It took some searching, but I landed on the perfect situation: a job as an entry-level graphic designer that required only 1.5 days a week in the office. Granted, one of those days was a fifteen-hour day, but I was off the following afternoon. It was perfect. Not only did it help slow my financial bleeding, it taught me a lot more about graphic design. I had already become familiar with it while working at the corporation, but this was a more hands-on position. I got to where I could easily work in Photoshop and InDesign, creating client-approved graphics for printed advertising. That experience was golden for my writing career, as I've continued to use those skills when working on my own website, advertisements, business cards, flyers, and more.

Instituting a plan C provided the best of both worlds—a solution I would never have discovered if I thought my only option was choosing between plan A and plan B. So if you feel stuck between two less-than-optimal choices, consider your own plan C. Start by first thinking about the options, then write them down in your journal, no matter how far-fetched they may seem. They might eventually evolve into workable solutions.

If I were to go with a plan C, I might:

1. _____

2 _____

3. _____

Making a Decision: Use Your Artistic Skills

Brainstorming and problem solving can be fun. You're talking about your business, after all. It's exciting to imagine what you might do with it and how you might improve it in the future.

Eventually, however, you have to stop all the thinking, considering, and talking and actually take that first step forward. That's where courage comes in. But clarity can be hard to find sometimes. You may want to take action, but fear you've made the wrong decision. That means it's time to give your analytical brain a break and try a new tactic.

Sometimes we can overthink situations, so it helps to allow the more artistic and imaginative right brain to have its say. When I was working at the corporation, I had to attend a boring meeting. I had been at the company for about three years and as I've mentioned, was considering leaving to freelance full-time. The decision was frightening enough to cause me to put off making any definite plans, but that day as I sat in that meeting, I doodled absentmindedly in my notebook. When I looked down, I saw that I had drawn a jet airplane taking off toward the edge of the paper. I realized then what my right brain was saying: *You need to get out of here! Now!* I left the company a few months later.

When you engage in any type of artistic activity, you use the power of the right brain, which can give you insights into your feelings. By freeing your mind and imagination, you may see more clearly what you need to do as a creative entrepreneur. So give your creative side a chance to talk to you without interference.

Finding Courage to Take That Leap

Pull out a blank piece of paper and a pen or pencil—whichever helps you feel more artistic—and set a timer (the one on your cell phone is fine) for sixty seconds.

Okay, pen or pencil at the ready, timer set, disregard any thoughts about whether or not you can draw because you're going to draw now—no excuses. Don't worry, no one but you will ever see it. Start the timer, then read the question below and immediately begin drawing. Don't hesitate. Don't think. Just let your hand do its thing. When the timer goes off, stop immediately.

The question:

How do you feel about your writing business right now?

Draw!

...

...

...

...

...

...

...

Ding!

Okay, the timer went off. Look at your drawing. Take time to analyze what it's telling you, and write down your feelings as they surface. See if this exercise helps you feel more or less confident about taking that risk you're considering.

Six Ways for Gaining Clarity on Your Decision

If you're still not sure whether you should take this risk or not, here are six more techniques you can use to gain clarity.

1. Determine the Urgency

Timing is everything. When I was thinking about quitting my job and going freelance, I knew the one thing I needed was a dependable three-to-six-months-income cushion in savings. Without the security of a corporate paycheck, I needed a safety net, so I set a dollar goal and started saving each month. This way when I reached that goal, I could turn in my two weeks notice, but not before.

Decide the best time to take this risk. Do you need to make a change right now or can you wait a few months? If you want to self-publish your next book, when should you begin? If you want to cut back on your work hours, when is the best time to start?

To gain clarity on this important step, complete the following exercise. You'll start by writing down a number between one and ten, with one being "not very strong" and ten being "super strong." Be ready to write this number down instantly in response to the following question:

How strong is your desire for change? _____

If you wrote down a number between eight and ten, you may need to step up your efforts so you can move on this risk sooner rather than later. If you wrote down a number between one and three, however, you can give yourself some time.

Using my example of taking out a loan, my urgency was a ten. I was desperate to make a change.

2. Utilize the three-brain decision-making process.
You can employ the three-brain decision-making process you learned in the last chapter to help you decide on this risk. Using your journal to record your answers, ask each brain whether or not you should go forward:

My gut says I should _____.

My heart says I should _____.

My head says I should _____.

If they don't all agree, then do more thinking. Remember, never go against your dominant brain!

For me, my gut and heart agreed to take the loan, but my head disagreed. Because my gut is my dominant brain, and the heart agreed (two out of three), I moved forward. I did listen to my head, though, and eventually got a part-time job to help with what it was worried about—finances.

3. Use your top two cognitive functions.
Look back to the top two cognitive functions you identified in chapter eight. Ask yourself if the risk you're considering will help you

build on your strengths and if the change will move you in a direction likely to fulfill your highest potential.

One of my top cognitive functions is introverted intuition (Ni). I'm naturally independent and entrepreneurial and find it easy to picture my future. Therefore, it made total sense for me to revive my business, as I knew that working for someone else would not make me happy, or serve my highest potential. I used my Ni strength to make the decision, and I've never regretted it.

The decision to go forward with a risk or not is determined by which lines up best with your top two cognitive strengths.

4. Be in a calm place.

Extreme emotions often result in bad decision making. Before deciding whether or not to go forward with this risk, make sure you are feeling calm, cool, and centered. Choose a day when life is happy and uncomplicated. You need a clear, unencumbered thought process. If you're preoccupied by an unhappy or traumatic event, you could decide not to go forward, which might be the wrong decision influenced by the wrong reasons.

Conversely, euphoria can also result in faulty decision making. If you decide on a day when your story wins a contest, you'll feel elated, like nothing can touch you. That sense of over-confidence has a good chance of coming back to bite you later.

Your best bet is to get away for a day or two in order to give yourself space to be more circumspect about the situation. Seeing the whole picture also allows you to leave the stress behind and think clearly about this important decision you're making.

5. Use your intuition.

If you rely on your intuition, use it to your advantage when gaining clarity on a risk. Present the question to yourself in a way that encourages a "yes" or "no" answer, something like this: "Should I take this risk?" Then forget about it and go about your life for a week. Don't actively seek out signs, but do pay attention to the feedback you get from yourself even in mundane daily life.

You see, our perceptions are highly influenced by what's going on inside us. If you're ecstatic because you got a publishing contract, everything looks sunny, even if it's raining outside, and if someone cuts in front of you on the road, you shrug and forgive them. If you just got a bad review on your book, however, things are likely to look much different. The rain will reflect your sour mood, and that person cutting you off may end up on the receiving end of your rage.

Here we're using your unconscious mind to stew over the question of whether or not to take this risk, and all you have to do is gauge whether what you perceive is mostly positive or mostly negative. Did you notice a pretty bird landing near your window and feel a moment's delight? Did you happen to spot a shiny quarter on the ground in the parking lot and pick it up? Or did you notice the rude barista at the coffee shop or get exasperated by your cluttered desk? Allow your intuition to communicate with you about your true feelings. Record your observations at night and see if they help give you clarity on your decision.

6. *Think more about what you'll gain rather than what you'll lose.*
Be aware that your brain will cling more tightly to what it thinks you'll lose than what you might gain. It's such an established human behavior that scientists have a name for it: loss aversion.

In a 2007 study out of the University of California, Los Angeles, researchers found that the brain's neural response to a potential loss, such as losing $100, was larger than the neural response to a potential gain, such as winning $100. In a gambling scenario, on average, people had to be offered the chance to earn nearly *twice as much* before they would consider risking what they had.

Other research has resulted in similar findings. In one interesting 2016 study, scientists decided to give participants a financial incentive to see if it might help them lose weight. They asked about 280 people interested in weight loss to walk at least seven thousand steps a day over a thirteen-week period. They were divided into three groups with three different financial incentives:

- **Group 1:** Each person received $1.40 for every day they hit the goal.

- **Group 2:** Each person was entered into a daily lottery, but was eligible to receive the reward only if he or she reached the goal the day before.

- **Group 3:** Each person was given $42 up front each month, but $1.40 was taken away each day the goal wasn't met.

Can you guess which group did the best when it came to sticking with their daily steps? Group three—the ones who risked losing money—exercised more than the other two groups. The idea of losing the money they already had in hand proved to be more motivating than either gaining money each day or chancing a daily lottery.

Keep this in mind as you consider taking a risk for your business. Your brain's tendency to cling more to what you might lose could cause you to overlook the very real potential gains. Give equal weight to both sides before making a decision.

Set a Deadline and Act!

After deciding to take this risk, set a tentative deadline and act. Trust yourself. You can do this. Even if it doesn't work out, you can recover, but it's better to give it a try than to remain stagnant. The important thing to understand is at some point, you're going to have to take a risk (and probably many risks) to move your business forward.

No matter how experienced you are, risk is always a little uncomfortable and a little scary. There's always going to be a certain level of uncertainty about the outcome because that's what risks are—they're uncertain. You can, however, increase your odds that the risk will turn out well. Don't let the decision hang over your head and keep you in a state of anxiety, as that will only sap the energy you need for your creative endeavors! Instead, decide, take action, and enjoy the ride.

Discover More: Get the Ball Rolling

It's time to put your decision into action, and it's critical you start right away. If you wait even a couple days, your fear may get the best of you, causing you to backtrack on your decision. Here's how to find your inner courage to move forward.

In your journal, write down the first three things you're going to do to make this change happen. These should be baby steps. Once I decided to take out my loan, I first considered all the options and then chose the best one. Then I signed the papers to get the money into my bank account and began taking action to attract new clients.

In your journal, list the steps you will take to get the ball rolling.

1. Step One: _____

2. Step Two: _____

3. Step Three: _____

If you decided *not* to take a risk right now, but still feel like you need to make a small change, brainstorm to see what you can do to prepare for taking this risk at some future date. Perhaps you can study on the side to increase your skills, start a special savings account, or put together an action plan for moving forward when the time is right.

Alternative/preparatory tasks to complete:

_____

_____

CHAPTER 16

YOUR WRITING
LABORATORY

L YDIA WAS EXCITED. She'd done a lot of thinking and brain-storming about her writing business and realized what she really wanted to focus on was women's relationships. Her books were all about women and their friends, sisters, mothers, and daughters, so it seemed fitting. It was a rich topic, so she wasn't sure what her niche might be, but when she started researching her strengths, she realized that her top two cognitive functions were Ne (extroverted intuiting—seeing connections) and Fi (introverted feeling—empathizing). With that in mind, she brainstormed some ideas and landed on the following theme:

Exploring the Mystical Bonds Between Women

The theme felt right, as Lydia's books were not only about women, but women in fantasy stories, so the "mystical" fit perfectly. "Bonds" worked with her strengths of seeing connections and empathizing. As for her blog, she thought she'd focus on the following topic categories:

- stories of mythical female friendships

- rituals and celebrations women could do together

- handmade gifts women could exchange

- how-to articles about overcoming challenges in female relationships

It took her a while to land on a title for this blog, but she finally came up with:

Treasure Her

She even found the domain "TreasureHer.com" was available. Nothing was holding her back now from trying out this new idea to see what might happen. She went through her website hosting company and found she could buy the domain for only about $25, but instead of jumping on the opportunity, she closed down the website and decided to think about it.

As we now know, that was a bad move. Another day passed, and another, and still Lydia didn't take action. Fear—specifically, fear of making a mistake—took over. James Hayton, Professor of Entrepreneurship at Warwick Business School, and Gabriella Cacciotti, Assistant Professor at Warwick Business School, interviewed sixty-five entrepreneurs to find out how fear affected them. (Remember, as a writer, you are an entrepreneur!) Some had established businesses and some were just starting out. The professors found those who worried about the viability of their ideas, or about their ability to develop those ideas, were more likely to suffer from fear's negative consequences. They got stuck in analysis paralysis, became less proactive, and found it difficult to make the decisions that would move them forward.

This chapter is all about changing your mindset. Instead of imagining yourself as a writer, and every project as the final word on your creative capability, imagine yourself as a scientist and each of your projects are simple experiments. Your goal is to learn what works and what doesn't, so let's get into your laboratory and have some fun!

Let Your Writing Nook Be Your Laboratory

As a writer, it's easy to get caught up in whether or not your idea is going to work. Is this the *best* idea you could come up with? Will this idea grant you the success you're looking for? The problem is, you'll never know the answer until you try.

Entrepreneurs of all types know they must take action on an idea before they can decide to keep going or to change direction. Looking back, I remember many times I took way too long analyzing an idea to death when I should have just given it a whirl. Today I'm much more likely to try new things because I've done it enough that it no longer scares me.

Could you make a mistake? Sure. Might your idea turn out to be less than awesome? Maybe. It doesn't matter. You just need to try it. Put your business hat on and be brave. It matters less than you think whether the idea works out perfectly. What matters more is the experience of trying it, implementing it, seeing how it goes, and then adjusting course as you need to.

William R. Kerr and colleagues note in their article published in the *Journal of Economic Perspectives*: "Entrepreneurship is fundamentally about experimentation because the knowledge required to be successful cannot be known in advance or deduced from some set of first principles." In other words, you can't know how your idea (or book, or post, etc.) will turn out until you try it. "For entrepreneurs," they continue, "it can be virtually impossible to know whether a particular technology or product or business model will be successful, until one has actually invested in it."

You can't get away from the fact that you're going to have to bite the bullet, invest the money and time, and see where this idea takes you. Imagine your writing nook as your laboratory, and you are the scientist conducting an experiment. If fear is still holding you back, shrink the size of your experiment to fine-tune your idea. Lydia could take her new theme to her writing group, for example, and ask them what they think of it. Better yet, she could put together a group of themes she's thought about and then gather some opinions on them.

She could use social media for this purpose, too, or create a survey on her website. She could ask her readers if they would get more out of posts about relationships between mothers and daughters or about historical relationships between women. She could list five possible post titles in each category and ask readers to choose the ones they'd most like to read. Or she could provide a snippet from two different posts and ask them to choose.

When I was looking for a title for my last book, *Overwhelmed Writer Rescue*, I spent months brainstorming and finally whittled it down to four I liked. I then sent these four out to ten writing friends and asked them to tell me which they liked best and why. Boy, was that helpful! Through that experiment, I realized that none of my titles were quite right. The one I'd thought was perfect wasn't getting the feedback I thought it would, and no one title was standing out from the others. Further, my friends' responses to "why" gave me a lot of information about what readers were really looking for, and what they thought they'd find in the book based on the title.

So I went back to the drawing board. I brainstormed some more. Then one night, the final title came to me. When it did, I felt pinpricks all over my skin. I knew I'd finally landed on the right one. Still, I used an online application to gather opinions about it and the one other I was still considering. This time, the votes leaned heavily in favor of the one I liked, and I was finally able to move on with publication.

You can use small experiments like these, too, to help identify your best step forward. Not only are they fun to do, but they'll give you useful information for your projects, and even your niche, as you'll begin to find out what your readers are really looking for.

Evaluate the Outcomes

Once you implement your idea (or your mini-experiment), you'll want to evaluate how it worked. You need this information to continue to build your career and your audience.

- **Does this idea feel right?** The main thing to focus on here is your energy level. If it's high, the idea is probably working. If it's low, not so much.

- **Do your readers like it?** Did your experiment attract more readers? What did people say about your new website/posts/tweets/books? Evaluate the comments and try to get a bird's-eye view of what they're telling you about this idea.

- **Is there room to improve?** Even if the idea turned out way better than you'd hoped, there are always areas where you can improve.

- **Do you want to keep going?** Use this as the litmus test for your new idea. Do you want to keep moving forward with it, or does it feel like it's just not working?

Let's say Lydia goes through the entire process of hiring a designer, discussing the new website, and getting the project done. She has a logo for *Treasure Her,* her new blog, and she spends about six months writing twice-weekly posts for it. These posts are about all the topics she brainstormed, but they also include regular features on real women who share the challenges they've experienced in relationships. She also gives away an article entitled "Ten Ways to Create a Lasting Friendship with Your Sister" to entice new people to sign up for her newsletter, which focuses on the same theme. Finally, she writes a couple guest posts, too, and gets them published on other blogs that focus on women's relationships.

Six months later, she decides to take stock of how her idea is playing out. By using Google Analytics on her website, she can see that her readership is up. She has an average of one-thousand more visits per month now than she had when she started. Her newsletter sign-ups have also increased—not as much as she'd hoped, but she's getting a steady stream of new subscribers. Her social media posts are receiving more attention, too, with more likes and retweets.

As Lydia analyzes these statistics, she sees that her new idea is working well. Perhaps the biggest indication is that in the process of writing all these posts, she's come up with an idea for a new nonfiction book on how to foster healthy female friendships. Lydia feels more alive and more creative than she's ever felt in her life. She knows she's on the right course, and though she wants to do some problem solving on how to get more subscribers, she feels like she's definitely found her niche.

But it doesn't always work out this perfectly. Lydia could have tried to write posts on her theme and gotten stuck. She may have written three and then struggled to find a fourth topic. Maybe the number of visits to her website stayed the same or dropped, or her social media posts continued to be largely ignored. By the end of the six months, she may have felt it was just not working, and that she needed to try something else.

If that happens, it's okay. Lydia learned a lot by implementing this idea. All she has to do now is go through the process again, using what she's learned. She can look for positive reader feedback on her posts. If she doesn't have any feedback, she can brainstorm some other ideas, and perform some mini-experiments with those ideas among her writing friends. Perhaps she can research other sites that follow a similar theme, and see what women are talking about.

One of the most important things she can do is to ask herself one question: "What problem are my readers trying to solve?"

Attending to the Reader's Needs

Too often writers stay stuck in their own points of view. After all, writing is a solitary endeavor and when we apply the same single-minded approach to blogging and marketing, the results can be disappointing.

I see hundreds of blogs where the writer is obviously stuck in her own world. She's writing about what happened in her day, or how far along she is on her story, or what her son did when he got home from school. There's nothing wrong with sharing personal stories now and then, but it's not the type of thing readers are going to seek out over and over again. They need something that applies to them and their lives.

Think about what you look for when you read blogs or browse the Internet. Sure, you enjoy the occasional story about a person's family, but if you're pressed for time (like most of us are), you're probably going to gravitate toward information that's going to *help* you, right? It's important to keep that in mind when thinking about what to offer others on your website, blog, social media pages, or YouTube channel. The more you can address topics that appeal to many of your readers, the more they will be inclined to come back to you for more.

What problem are your readers trying to solve? Lydia may find her readers really struggle with certain facets of mother-daughter relationships. Or maybe they get stuck when it comes to overcoming challenges with their sisters. Maybe they need more ideas on things to do with their female friends or advice on gifts to exchange. Or maybe Lydia discovers something unexpected—that her readers are super-interested in more mystical subjects, like the power of crystals in relationships or tapping into deeper intuitive powers. Since all of these topic areas fall under her theme, and thus relate to the writing she does, they're all possible avenues for her to explore.

This is why it's so helpful to establish a blog (and an email newsletter). It gives you a way to experiment with different topics and themes, and as you start attracting readers, you can ask them what they're looking for. Run a survey and give something away to entice people to respond. Write a post on each of the categories you're considering, and then see which one gets the most readers (using Google

Analytics). There are so many ways to get feedback, and the more you know about what your tribe is looking for, the more you can give it to them.

Be Open to Change

Even after you find your niche and start growing your platform, realize that you may experience changes along the way. Opportunities may open up for you, or your muse may want to go in a slightly different direction. Your skills will grow, too, and you may see a new angle you can take on your theme.

Discard the old notion of what a writer is "supposed" to be. Yes, you are a writer, but if you want to sell your work, you're also an entrepreneur. You're in business for yourself. If you want to create a site that helps women craft gifts for other women, go for it! Who knows? You could eventually make good money writing and publishing books about the topic.

I know a talented writer who does beadwork. She travels to conferences talking to other women interested in the craft and teaches them how to make beautiful pieces of jewelry. She's also published three books on the topic that are popular among bead enthusiasts and is working on a fourth.

Your passion will take you far if you're willing to open up your writing laboratory and begin experimenting.

Discover More: Your First Mini-Experiment

Let's take a new idea and try it as a mini-experiment. First, think about the kind of experiment you want to conduct—maybe an online survey sent by email to a few friends asking for their opinions, or a series of new blog posts for which you'll track reader response. Using your journal, write down your experiment.

My Mini-Experiment:

_____

Now write down what you want to discover with this experiment. Maybe you want to figure out your best title, your best book cover, what topics your readers are most interested in, or what niche or author theme sounds most interesting.

What I Want to Discover is:

_____

Now go conduct your experiment, and then come back to record your results.

Based on my experiment, I should:

_____

CHAPTER 17

THE LONG VIEW

MY FAMILY USED to take road trips from Colorado to New York once a year to visit my grandmother. We'd pack up the truck or station wagon—whichever we had at the time—with cans of food, water, sleeping bags, and a boom box, and set out on America's highways. Many times we drove straight through, as hotels were expensive. My parents would trade off driving, and later, as we kids got old enough, we'd take our turn at the wheel.

Occasionally we'd stop at a presidential museum to look around and hopefully learn something or eat a warm meal at a café, but most of the time we found ways to entertain ourselves in the vehicle. We played road games like "I Spy" or tried filling up a country map with license plates we spotted from each state. We blasted Oak Ridge Boys on the boom box—either because we were in the back of the truck away from the radio or because the radio didn't work—and sang "Elvira" at the top of our lungs. We ate on the go, popping open cans of Beanie Weenies and spaghetti and making sandwiches out of bread and deviled ham.

Looking back, I can see how magical those trips were, but at the time, I remember wanting one thing: to get there. Though we weren't stupid enough to shout "Are we there yet?" (my parents weren't the types to tolerate demanding kids), we were definitely thinking it. We each brought things to keep us entertained, but let's face it—after twelve, twenty-four, thirty-six-plus hours in a vehicle, you tend to go a little stir crazy, and the one thing you want desperately is to arrive!

As writers and artistic entrepreneurs, we often feel the same way. We need to get where we're going, and we need to get there now. But building a career takes time, often years. It's not something you can do in six months. Talk to any successful author or business owner and you'll hear how success is built on reputation and a readership—neither of which is accomplished quickly.

Building a Writing Career Takes Time

I've spoken with a lot of young writers who were chomping at the bit to write that one hit that would bring them instant success. They were convinced that finding the right agent or editor would result in that big publishing contract and after that, the good life.

I'm assuming, if you've read this far in the book, you know this scenario is a myth. Even if you're fortunate enough to land a contract with one of the few remaining big publishers, you're still responsible for establishing a niche and building a readership. That means it's important to take the long view of your career. Settle in and get ready to build it a little every day.

I wish someone had told me this early on. I kept thinking I had to get to a point—and soon—where I could quit my day job (as a freelance writer) and focus solely on the books I wanted to write. I spent a lot of time feeling like a failure because things weren't moving as quickly as I thought they should.

I realize now that I made a few mistakes. It took me way too long to figure out my niche, for one. I hope this book helps you find yours much sooner. I also didn't realize building a readership was my responsibility, and that it would take time. In other words, I should have started way earlier than I did.

I'm assuming you already have a regular writing practice in place. Either you're writing every day or you have some other similar schedule that gets the words down on the page in a consistent manner. Now you need to start incorporating the other activities necessary to building your author brand into your daily life. This is where it can become challenging, as so many authors will tell you, because there can be so much to do that you begin to feel overwhelmed trying to get to it all.

My advice is to break it up. Set aside one night a week to write a blog and perhaps one lunch hour to write your newsletter. Choose one day a month to work on your next freebie. Decide to update your website this summer. The options for how you schedule these tasks into your week or month or year are practically endless. What matters is that you put in time on a regular basis not just on your writing, but on your platform activities too.

Seven Basic Steps to Building a Lasting Author Brand

The following are the most important steps to creating a readership and establishing your expertise. You may add to this list or replace any of the steps depending on your niche. If something is working for you—a YouTube channel, podcast, or speaking circuit—don't hesitate to capitalize on it.

1. Blog Regularly in a Way That Supports Your Author Brand

At one time, writers debated about whether a blog was really necessary. I can tell you that my blog, *Writing and Wellness*, has opened many doors for me as a writer and an entrepreneur that I never expected. It helped establish me as an expert in my niche, gave me visibility, led to new writing projects that were successful, and even resulted in out-of-the-blue invitations for speaking engagements. As the website gradually extends its reach, I continue to gain new opportunities from it. Today, it is the platform I use to grow my readership and draw attention to my books and other projects. On top of that, it's a lot of fun.

The great thing about a blog is it's a low-investment project that can create a high level of return in terms of visibility. I host my own site, so I pay a yearly cost, but it's minimal considering how much I get in return. Blogging regularly (I post two-to-three times a week) and purposely inside your theme is one of the best ways to establish a presence online that attracts readers to you. I think it's *the* best way to do that.

A blog also gives you a place to regularly showcase your work. As a freelance writer, whenever I'm communicating with a potential client, I always include clips from my own website as well as from others I've written for. So even if you're not writing books, but you're a grant writer, editor, tech writer, or journalist, your own personal blog can serve as a great reference for you.

Realize that a blog is a long-term commitment. Particularly in the first year, you may feel like you're shouting into the wind. But as long as you're putting out good, valuable content that consistently benefits your readers, you'll build a library of information that will eventually get Google's attention—and your readers' too.

2. Support Your Blog with Your Social Media Channels

When you post on social media you need something to post *about*. Pictures of what you had for lunch or your dog's latest antics may be cute and can add some personal touches to your posts, but if that's all you've got, you need to offer something of value—and quickly—before your readers stray. Your blog, if done well, offers the perfect solution.

Producing a blog that fits within your theme usually results in posts that are evergreen—you can feature them on social media for years to come. I have about four years' worth of posts now that I can regularly talk about, so my social media platforms become reliable sources of helpful information for my readers. They know if they're struggling with any of the issues I cover, they can find answers in my Twitter posts or by following me on LinkedIn.

Of course, the purpose of social media is to be social, so feel free to share those pictures of your cat making a funny face whenever you'd like. But your posts need to be primarily about the helpful information you're offering. Then let your social media drive traffic to your blog and website. If you use social media correctly, it will help to establish both your brand and your expertise, so readers know exactly what to expect when they come to you.

Just like blogging regularly, you need to post regularly to your social media channels. Get a scheduling app like Hootsuite, HubSpot, or TweetDeck and set up posts to go out at least three times a day. I take about an hour each week to schedule my posts, then I don't worry about it the rest of the week.

265

There are programs like Social Jukebox, Buffer, and Missinglettr that will automatically pull posts from your blog. The danger is if you simply allow an app to spew out content all the time, your social media platforms will start to appear mechanical. Readers will pick up on this and likely lose interest. The important thing is to schedule at least a couple posts a week that appear more personal. Then make sure to interact with people—comment on their posts, say "hi," and share other posts—at least once a week (it doesn't have to be every day).

3. Send Out a Quality Newsletter on a Consistent Schedule

Any writer or entrepreneur today will tell you how critical an email list is. Your subscribers are the people who have signed up to hear what you have to say, and they are golden to your author business. That means two things:

- you need to keep growing your list as much as you can

- you need to treat these people really well

I see authors who overwhelm, ignore, or irritate their email subscribers. Don't be one of them. These actions can be deadly to any writing career. First, it's extremely important to establish a schedule and *stick with it* so readers know when to expect emails, and then you stay visible and relevant without irritating them. I've found in my business that a once-weekly email works great. It's enough that people enjoy them, and not so much that they feel overwhelmed.

Neither do you want to wait so long between your newsletters that people forget about you. Remember you want to maintain your expertise in your readers' eyes—that's what they came to you for—so it's important to continue sending your best readers helpful information. Design a schedule that fits your readership and commit to it, but don't wait too long between emails. Twice a month is best when starting out, and then build to once a week when needed.

Second, don't abuse your readers. Your newsletter is about helping them, maintaining your visibility, and reaffirming your expertise. Of course, you're going to want to sell your books or other products eventually, but if you focus mainly on that (and I've seen many authors do this), you're going to irritate your subscribers, and they'll either ignore you or unsubscribe. Consider how you like to be treated as a subscriber, and that will help you maintain the right balance.

None of us wants to spend valuable time reading advertisements. It can also make you feel used if every time you read a newsletter, the author is trying to get something from you. Be sure that no matter what else you put in your newsletter, you have valuable, helpful information that fits your author theme.

4. Frequently Create New Freebies to Build Your Email List

The best way to attract new subscribers to your newsletter is to offer them something of value in exchange for an email address. The subscriber is inviting you into his or her online "home," so to speak, so arrive at the door with a gift! It's only polite, right?

You'll need to invest some time into creating a freebie your readers will enjoy. Again, make sure it fits with your author theme. As noted earlier, on her blog *Treasure Her*, our friend Lydia gives away a free article entitled "Ten Ways to Create a Lasting Friendship with Your Sister." She might also give away free instructions on how to create a special friendship necklace or bracelet, or an article entitled "10 Tips to Resolve Any Disagreement with Your Best Friend."

You may decide to give away a short story, or a free chapter of your book. Before you do this, think carefully because if you give away either, you're really trying to entice your reader to buy more of your work. There's nothing wrong with that in principle, but your reader is likely to sense your intent is to get something *from* her rather than giving something *to* her. You'll get more subscribers if you give away something of value along with your sample chapter or short story. Not that your work isn't valuable, but your reader doesn't know that yet, so until she does, you need to entice her with something that's clearly helpful. That way, she knows she's getting something free and clear in exchange for her email address, whether she likes your story or not.

A free short story can also fail as a freebie if your readers have yet to decide if they like your work. In most cases, people who are first-time visitors to your website haven't decided that yet. They may be curious enough about your writing to give it a shot, but then again, you'd probably be more successful if you offered a freebie that helped your reader solve a problem.

Most people are inundated with emails already, so it's important they believe you're going to provide them with something of high value. Think of what you'd be more likely to give up your time for—a short story by an author you've never heard of or something that helps you in your life? Most of us would choose the latter, so consider that when creating your freebies. You can always give away a short story, too, as once your reader absorbs the report or recipe or craft instructions or whatever you give away, he or she will probably be more open to reading your story.

Finally, commit to working on a new freebie on a regular basis. If you create just one freebie and then leave it up on your site year after year, it will get stale and new sign-ups will slow. Updating keeps your site fresh and also helps you keep track of which freebies really work for your audience. Every time you create a freebie, post about it on social media, and then you can track how readers respond. Voilà, you're doing market research! Put out four freebies per year on various topics within your theme, and the one or two that really stand out (that won you the most subscribers) will help you determine what your readers really want. Then you can start to respond to that desire with other products (freebies, posts, guest posts, e-books, courses) that fit into that category.

Freebies also help you generate content you can use later. Maybe you can combine some to create a new nonfiction book, online course, or end-of-the-year mega-free offering for your newsletter drive. Those freebies that didn't work well may end up in the back of your computer drive never to be opened again, but even those gave you valuable information you can use to build your business.

If you've never created a freebie, simply go to other writing, blogging, and online business sites and see what they do. Sign up for their email lists and download the freebies and see what they look like. (You can always unsubscribe later.) Save them in a folder for later reference. Then as you start to build your blog, use Google Analytics to see which posts are getting the most attention. Choose a topic and write about it. One of the things my readers struggle with, for example, is self-confidence, so I wrote a report entitled, "Seven Easy & Effective Ways to Increase Your Writer's Confidence." I created a simple design, inserted a few images, added a few pull quotes, saved it as a PDF, and then offered it up as a freebie.

Don't be afraid of making mistakes. Being an entrepreneur is all about experimentation (as we talked about in the last chapter). Just get something together and get it out there, then start working on your next freebie.

5. Guest Post

Guest posting works magic for your business if you do it right. Follow these steps:

- Find other blogs that fit in your niche. They don't have to be writing blogs. They just need to fit your theme.

- Write an article and pitch it to the other blog. Read their guidelines and some of the other blogs they've posted to be sure you know how to write for them.

- **Important!** At the end of your article, add a couple lines telling the reader that if she wants more information on the subject, she can come to your website and get her *free* report (your freebie), then add the website link.

- Query the blog to see if they may be open to your article. If so, submit the best post you can. If they aren't, move on to the next one.

- Direct your readers to the published post on social media and on your website (with a widget or short blog of your own).

- Always stay within your author theme or brand and offer the reader something of value at the end of your article. Interested readers can click the link to your site. If they like your freebie, they may sign up for your newsletter.

I've had good success getting new email subscribers using this process. I wish I would have known about it sooner, though, because I invested a lot of energy writing guest posts that didn't have the offer at the end. There's nothing wrong with that—it can help establish your expertise in your niche—but it doesn't get you email subscribers, and that's where the gold is as far as your author business is concerned.

If you make room in your regular schedule for guest posting (writing one or two a month, for example), you can start to make real headway increasing your subscribers. If it sounds overwhelming, realize that all you're doing is writing an extra blog post, then finding another blog that would be happy to publish it.

6. Keep Your Website Current

You can have the best content in the world, but if your website looks out of date, if it lacks engaging images, if it doesn't appear correctly on a cell phone or tablet, or if it loads too slowly, you're going to lose readers. People have a *lot* of websites to choose from. If your website doesn't attract them when they first arrive, they'll leave. At the very least, you need prominent headlines, attractive images, and easy-to-read text.

One pet peeve I have is when the text on a website is so small I have to enlarge it just to be able to read the words. Another annoyance is when the text is in all caps because it feels like I'm being shouted at. You want readers to *read* your posts, so the least you can do is make that reading experience easy and enjoyable. Using fancy fonts, particularly scripts, turns readers off, as do dark colors behind text, and long blocks of text without paragraph breaks. Screen-reading is hard on the eyes, so choose a website theme that gives you a white or light background, has easy-to-read text, and prominent headlines.

Pay attention to your navigation too. Make sure when a reader lands on your website, he knows exactly where to go. You can find more about good website design online, but two critical recommendations are to: make your website clean and inviting; and keep it up to date. A couple years ago, most websites switched to being "mobile-friendly" so they were easier to read on cell phones and tablets. If you're still operating on an old theme, it could be that your site is not appearing well on other channels, which could hurt your readership. Pull it up on your cell phone or tablet and see if you can navigate easily and notice if the posts are friendly on the eyes. If you can't or they aren't, it's time for a new design.

Finally, please be sure to include a "Contact" button on your navigation area that provides a simple, straightforward way for readers to contact you *outside* of your social media channels. I can't tell you how many times I've wanted to contact an author to feature him or her on *Writing and Wellness*, and I had to give up. Some authors have no contact information at all, and some simply provide their social media platforms. But if I'm not on Facebook, for example (which I'm not), I can't contact them on Facebook, so that doesn't help.

Either give an email address (spell it out to avoid bots—Lydia at TreasureHer dot com) or use a contact plug-in on your site (like WordPress's Contact Bank).

7. Support Others in Your Niche

One of the most rewarding things I do on *Writing and Wellness* is to regularly feature other writers. I love doing it because:

- I learn from them

- I like supporting them

When you reach out to support others in your niche, you also benefit. Let's go back to Lydia. Her blog *Treasure Her* is all about women's relationships with other women. To support people in her niche, she may begin to interview and feature various women who fit into her theme. She could interview mothers and daughters, for example, and ask them a series of questions, such as how they get past disagreements, what makes their relationship special, how they support each other, and what activities help them bond. She may also interview sisters, employees with female bosses, lesbian couples, female coauthors, grandmothers and granddaughters, and more. She could interview other experts on female relationships, or those who create activities specifically for women to do together (leaders of quilting or book clubs, for example). She could post reviews of books on the subject. She could even support other authors writing about female relationships.

With each interview or review, Lydia will learn more about her theme, and dive deeper into this topic she's passionate about. At the same time, she'll be reaching out to others and sharing their stories, helping them feel special and honored. Through this process, month after month, year after year, she'll be creating a network of people who fit into her theme, which benefits everybody. Her reach extends beyond herself, and her work becomes more rewarding.

I've had authors come up to me at events and ask how to go about getting others to agree to appear on their blogs. It's super-easy. Just follow these steps:

- Find the person's email address, then email and ask. No one can shoot you for asking! Don't let fear stop you.

- Explain how you found the person, and then tell her what inspires you about her. Let her know that you'd love to feature her and her work on your website.

- Briefly describe who you are and what your work involves (your theme).

- Finally, invite her to do an interview with you. Include your website address so she can see other similar features, and then wish her the best.

- Once she agrees, send her a list of questions to answer, or call her if you prefer a phone interview. Ask her for an author photo, too, so readers can put a face with the name. If she has a website or social media channels, include those so readers can find out more about her if they wish.

- Promote your guest posts *at least* as much as you do your own. Not only is it the right thing to do, it will sow goodwill among your readers, as well as give your site more breadth and depth. Feature these posts on your newsletter. Let others know what these fabulous people are doing. Gradually, you'll start creating relationships that will support your career as you move forward.

You'd be surprised how many people would enjoy being featured on your site, no matter how large or small it is. Everyone likes to feel noticed and appreciated, and that's what you're doing with a guest feature.

And remember—each and every one of these activities supports your work as an author. The more people are paying attention to what you're doing, the bigger your audience when you release your next book, or the bigger your potential clientele (if you're a free-lancer). What counts is eyes on your website and on the other pieces of your platform. The more you have, the more that might notice the next service you offer or novel you publish.

Let Your Writing Lead to Fulfillment

In these ways and more, you can fashion a writing career that is unique, successful, and impactful. Just remember it will take time. By doing a little bit every day, you'll gradually begin to see the results of your efforts, and your motivation will increase. The more motivated you are, the more you'll be able to do … the sky's the limit.

Discover More:
Choose One Platform-Building Activity

Choose one of the seven steps above—the one you most need to grow your author platform right now—and commit to working on that step at least once every week for a month or more. If you already have all seven of these things humming along, choose another activity that fits your platform and will help expand your reach. Some examples include scheduling more speaking engagements, building your YouTube channel, surveying your newsletter subscribers (to find out more about what they need), starting a new podcast, or running a webinar. Choose the day and time that work best, and schedule a thirty-minute block (an hour is better, if you can) on your calendar. Then stick to it until the project is completed or the update meets your new standards.

Using your journal, write down the project you want to focus on, then break it down into a series of steps. If you want to increase the number of guest posts you write, for example, then your list of steps may look like this:

Steps to Increase Guest Posts

- Brainstorm list of ten topic ideas by (deadline)

- Research potential websites and choose five to query by (deadline)

- Send out all five queries by (deadline)

- Write one post every (set day of the week)

- When a query is accepted, send the post

- Have all five posts scheduled to appear on other sites by (deadline)

Setting up even a simple list like this can help you overcome inertia and move forward. Even if you think you're too busy to add another project, if you break it down into its smallest steps, you'll be amazed at what you can accomplish.

CHAPTER 18

WHERE YOU BELONG

BACK WHEN I first started writing, I never envisioned the writing platform I have now. Then, my vision was limited. I thought more about getting a novel published than anything else. Because all I could see in my future was a publishing contract, my actions were limited too. I focused solely on writing novels, oblivious to all the other things I should have been doing to build a platform and ultimately, to create a unique writing career for myself.

I'm not entirely to blame. Back when I started, self-publishing, the push for authors to shoulder most of the marketing, and the importance of social media were mere rumors on the writing grapevine. Even when I first caught wind of them, I didn't understand their importance, as like most of the writing community, I was still stuck in the way things had always been done. By the time I realized the importance of building an author platform, I already had two novels traditionally published. I had reached my goal, twice, but I didn't yet have what for me was the "perfect" writing career.

When I finally woke up to the realities of today's world, I made some changes. I started building a more solid online presence. I offered my readers useful information. I set goals that went beyond finishing my next book to extending my reach as a creative entrepreneur. At the time, I thought I *had* to do these things to support my novels. Never did I imagine they would help me build something far more fulfilling than I ever could have built writing novels alone.

It may seem strange to think that expanding one's thinking *beyond the writing itself* could lead to a greater sense of purpose. Of course, there's joy in the act of creation that fills our hearts and keeps us coming back to the writer's desk. But sometimes we forget that it's on the other side of that desk, where we interact with others, that we discover where we truly belong.

Would you continue to write without readers? You might. The craft in itself is rewarding, no doubt. But I know from experience if you find a way to reach more readers, you have more of a chance to grow, not only as a writer, but as a person.

Now that I've experienced what it's like to learn and grow in the service of a writing platform and career, I know more peace in the actual act of writing. In my earlier years, anxiety was one of my constant writing companions. He was always whispering in my ear, "Do you think it will be good enough? Will they want to publish it? You're probably just wasting your time." Getting a publishing contract helped a little bit, but it wasn't until I found my niche and started getting regular readers (via my platform) that the anxiety faded. He could no longer rile me up because I had found my place, and I felt secure within it.

There's something magical about finding where you belong. The key is focusing on your strengths and passions, and then finding a way to use those to benefit others. Your next book matters, but it's not the *only* thing that matters. If you look around, you'll see the world is asking you to expand your work as a creative individual.

How will you respond? What will your contribution be? I hope after completing this book, you have a better idea of how you'd answer these questions. Most of all, I hope you've now broadened your vision so you can begin to see a thriving, robust writing career ahead of you—one that challenges, motivates, and inspires you every day. I promise you—it's waiting for you. All you have to do is go get it.

Good luck!

NOTE FROM THE AUTHOR

Reviews are gold to authors. If you've enjoyed this book, please consider rating and reviewing it on Amazon.com and/or Goodreads.com.

To learn more about empowering your health, wellness, and creativity, sign up for the free *Writing and Wellness* newsletter at writingandwellness.com/newsletter. You'll gain access to inspirational and motivational posts, additional training, future books, and more.

For more information on creatively building a successful author career, sign up for the free *Writer CEO* newsletter at writerceo.com/newsletter. Read stories from real writers who are earning a living writing and editing and find out more about how to run your own author business.

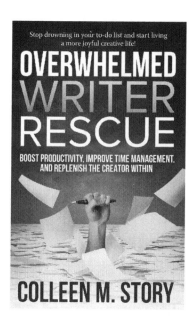

Are you drowning in your to-do list?

Do less important tasks frequently flood your schedule and sink your creative motivation?

Are you frustrated and out of touch with your inner artist?

Do you wish you could create a calmer, more creative life so you could write without guilt?

Your rescue is here!

Overwhelmed Writer Rescue

After twenty years' experience in the writing industry, author Colleen M. Story extends a lifeline to pull you out of the sinking swamp of "busyness" and back into the flourishing creative life you deserve.

Overwhelmed Writer Rescue provides practical, personalized solutions to help beginning and experienced writers and other creative artists escape the tyranny of the to-do list to nurture the genius within. You'll find ways to boost productivity, improve time management, and restore your sanity while gaining insight into your unique creative nature and what it needs to thrive.

Ultimately, you'll discover what may be holding you back from experiencing the true joy that a creative life can bring.

Available now on **Amazon** and wherever books are sold!

FEATURED AUTHORS

Listed in order of appearance are the authors who contributed their stories to this book. I offer my gratitude to each one of you!

Maryanne Pope is the author of *A Widow's Awakening*, the playwright of *Saviour*, and the screenwriter for *God's Country*. She was the executive producer of the documentary *Whatever Floats Your Boat ... Perspectives on Motherhood*. Maryanne is the founder & CEO of Pink Gazelle Productions, Inc. as well as chair of the John Petropoulos Memorial Fund (jpmf.ca). She lives on Vancouver Island in Canada. For more information or to subscribe to her blog, *Weekly Words of Wisdom*, please visit pinkgazelle.com. Find her book, *A Widow's Awakening*, at pinkgazelle.com/a-widows-awakening/.

Angelique L'Amour was born in Los Angeles, California. The daughter of author Louis L'Amour, she grew up in the household of a prolific writer where writing and storytelling were a way of life. She began writing for personal enjoyment as a child and went on to college to pursue a history degree. She also studied at the University of Southern California in the School of Journalism and while there wrote and published a volume of quotes from her father's works. Published by Bantam Doubleday Dell in 1988, *A Trail of Memories* spent sixteen weeks on the *New York Times* bestseller list and became a *Publishers Weekly* bestseller for the year. For more information, see Angelique's website at angeliquelamour.com and sign up for her newsletter at angeliquelamour.com/25-questions.

Sandy Fussell has Australian and international publication credits that include poetry, short stories, fiction, and nonfiction. Her greatest writing love is children's literature, which she discovered as a mother facing the challenge of boys who didn't want to read. Her novel *Polar Boy* was shortlisted for Australian Children's Book of the Year, and her Samurai Kids series received an international award for stories about disability. Her picture book *Sad the Dog* was reviewed in the *New York Times*. She is an Information and Communication Technologies consultant, book reviewer for a national newspaper, and one course short of a Math degree. Sandy is often found in a school library waving her practice sword or teaching a Minecraft-based writing workshop. Having survived three life-threatening illnesses in recent years, she knows for certain the glass is always half-full. For more information, please see her website at sandyfussell.com or follow her on Twitter (@sandyfussell).

Jeri Walker grew up in the eccentric mining town of Wallace, Idaho. A bipolar mother, spousal abandonment, and breast cancer shaped her into a resilient soul and raconteur of personal upheaval and wanderlust. *Lost Girl Road* (in progress) is a work of contemporary psychological fiction set in the woods of northwest Montana. An appreciation for travel, minimalism, personal growth, and human conditioning are reflected in her writing. Her creative nonfiction and short stories have been published in *Idaho Magazine* and *cold-drill*, the literary and arts journal at Boise State University. Most recently, she won first place in the 2018 Idaho Writers Guild essay contest. Sign up for her quarterly author newsletter at bit.ly/JeriWalker, or find her on Amazon at amzn.to/2D8lshw.

Alexandria Szeman is the author of several award-winning books including the *New York Times Book Review* Notable Book & Top 100 Books of the Year *The Kommandant's Mistress*, which also won the Kafka Award for "outstanding book of prose fiction by an American woman." Poems in her collections *Love in the Time of Dinosaurs* and *Where Lightning Strikes: Poems on the Holocaust* were awarded the Elliston Poetry Prize, and her short story collection *Naked, with Glasses* won the UKA Press Grand Prize. Alexandria's true crime memoir *M is for Munchers: The Serial Killers Next Door* was a finalist in the Santa Fe Writer's Project Literary Awards 2017. She is a writer at *The Mighty* and *The Migraine Mantras*. For more information, please see her Amazon author page at amazon.com/Alexandria-Constantinova-Szeman/e/B007TTLXS8/ref=sr_ntt_srch_lnk_1?qid=1546148495&sr=1-1.

Linda Osmundson is the author of hundreds of nonfiction articles for children and adults. She authored three books in the *How the West Was Drawn* series for ages 7 to 107 (the award-winning *Cowboy Charlie's Art*, *Frederic Remington's Art*, and the award-winning *Women's Art*). She lives in beautiful Fort Collins, Colorado, with a view of the Rocky Mountains and Long's Peak from her deck. For more information, please see her website at www.LindaOsmundson.com or connect with her on Facebook at facebook.com/linda. osmundson.52.

Troy Lambert is a freelance writer and author who lives, works, and plays in Boise, Idaho. He writes for the tech and business industries and pens suspense thriller novels. At heart, he is a researcher and storyteller, and his goal is to make the world a better place through both sharing stories and helping others share theirs. He's currently working on a nonfiction book, *Writing as a Business: Production, Distribution, and Marketing*, as well as several fiction pieces scheduled to release in 2019. You can find Troy on your favorite social media platform or at unboundnorthwest.com. You can also find him on LinkedIn (linkedin.com/in/troy-lambert/).

Megan Cutler grew up in a small town in central Pennsylvania where books offered an easy escape from the mundane life of a rural highway town. In 2003 she married the love of her life and moved to Canada. Megan started writing full time in 2011 and has since published five novels and several short stories, including the Mystical Island Trilogy. Her characters keep her up late and wake her up early, but she loves them anyway. For more information, please visit her website at megancutler.net/ or her Amazon author page at amazon. com/Megan-Cutler/e/B00KDPQAF6/.

Laurie Buchanan, PhD, is a board-certified holistic health practitioner, life coach, and award-winning author who helps others turn intention into action. A cross between Dr. Dolittle, Nanny McPhee, and a type-A Buddhist, Laurie is a voracious reader, award-winning author, kindness enthusiast, and an unabashed optimist. Her first book, *Note to Self: A*

Seven-Step Path to Gratitude and Growth, closes the gap between where you are and where you want to be. Her second book, *The Business of Being: Soul Purpose in and Out of the Workplace*, shows you how to thrive, soul-side out, in and out of the workplace. Find more information on Laurie's website at TuesdaysWithLaurie.com.

Cindy Helms is a visual artist, author, and illustrator. Her artwork includes acrylic, graphic design, and pencil drawings. After many years as an IT manager, another many years as a stay-at-home mom, and yet another many years designing and building sets for musical theater, Cindy has set her artistic self free with the publication of several award-winning children's books: *Outside, Inside; Who's New; Polygonsters; Honk Whoop;* and *100 Things*. She has degrees from DePauw University and the University of Denver and continues to study, read, and write reviews for the *New York Journal of Books*. For more information, please see her website at cindyhelms.com, or her reviewer page at the *New York Journal of Books* (nyjournalofbooks.com/reviewer/cindy-helms).

Natalie Cline Bright is an author and blogger. Her stories and articles have appeared in numerous publications. She enjoys talking to all ages about writing. Her chapter book adventure Trouble in Texas series for ages 8–10 is set in the Texas frontier. Her easy reader Rescue Animal series is about second chances for rescue horses, and she also writes women's fiction. Natalie blogs about story craft at Wordsmith-Six Blogspot and posts articles about the people, places, and history of the Texas Panhandle at Prairie Purview. For more information, please see her website at nataliebright.com, or follow her on Instagram (instagram.com/natsgrams/).

Linda K. Sienkiewicz writes about ordinary people on extraordinary journeys. Her short stories, poetry, and art have been published in more than fifty literary journals and anthologies. Among her awards are five finalist awards for her debut novel *In the Context of Love*, a Pushcart Prize nomination, and a poetry chapbook award from Heartlands. She has an MFA from the University of Southern Maine. Find more information on her website at lindaksienkiewicz.com.

Jennifer Bernard is a *USA Today* bestselling author of contemporary romance. Her books have been called "an irresistible reading experience" full of "quick wit and sizzling love scenes." A graduate of Harvard and former news promo producer, she left big city life for true love in Alaska, where she now lives with her husband and stepdaughters. She still hasn't adjusted to the cold, so most often she can be found cuddling with her laptop and a cup of tea. For more information, see her website at JenniferBernard.net or sign up for her newsletter at eepurl.com/bN8UMn.

REFERENCES

Chapter 1

Jesionka, N. (2012, November 23). Embrace Your Paths: Why Having Multiple Jobs is a Good Thing. Retrieved from https://www.themuse.com/advice/embrace-your-paths-why-having-multiple-jobs-is-a-good-thing

Chapter 2

Barber, R. (2016, March 15). Authors and the Truth About Money - Ros Barber. Retrieved from http://rosbarber.com/authors-truth-money/

Publisher's Weekly. (2014, January 15). DBW 2014: Survey Finds Most Authors Want to Earn More. Retrieved from https://www.publishersweekly.com/pw/by-topic/digital/content-and-e-books/article/60644-dbw-2014-survey-finds-most-authors-want-to-earn-more.html

Chapter 3

Friedman, J. (2018, July 16). A Definition of Author Platform | Jane Friedman. Retrieved from https://www.janefriedman.com/author-platform-definition/

Fussell, S. (2018, January 3). Featured Writer on Wellness: Sandy Fussell | Writing and Wellness. Retrieved from http://www.writingandwellness.com/2018/01/03/featured-writer-on-wellness-sandy-fussell/

L'Amour, A. (2018, August 15). Chemo, Cupcakes and Carpools: How to Parent Positively Through Cancer | Writing and Wellness. Retrieved from http://www.writingandwellness.com/2018/08/15/how-to-parent-positively-through-cancer/

Pope, M. (2017, November 1). Tragedy Was My Inspiration to Write | Writing and Wellness. Retrieved from http://www.writingandwellness.com/2017/11/01/tragedy-was-my-inspiration-to-write/

Chapter 4

Szeman, A. (2018, February 1). Featured Writer on Wellness: Alexandria Constantinova Szeman | Writing and Wellness. Retrieved from http://www.writingandwellness.com/2018/02/01/featured-writer-on-wellness-alexandria-constantinova-szeman/

Walker, J. (2017, February 22). Featured Writer on Wellness: Jeri Walker | Writing and Wellness. Retrieved from http://www.writingandwellness.com/2017/02/22/featured-writer-on-wellness-jeri-walker/

Chapter 5

Brown, A. B. (2017, March 11). Academic Writing Success | Academic Writing Coach Reviews. Retrieved from https://academiccoachingandwriting.org/academic-writing/academic-writing-blog/v-the-importance-of-recognizing-your-strengths-as-a-writer

Brown, P. B. (2013, July 7). Forget About Working On Your Weaknesses, Play To Your Strengths. A Case Study. Retrieved from https://www.forbes.com/sites/actiontrumpseverything/2013/07/07/forget-about-working-on-your-weaknesses-play-to-your-strengths-a-case-study/#18be1d893e2d

Christchurch City Libraries Blog. (2009, August 11). David Eddings R.I.P. Retrieved from https://cclblog.wordpress.com/2009/06/04/david-eddings-r-i-p/

Hanson, R. (2010, October 26). Confronting the Negativity Bias. Retrieved from https://www.psychologytoday.com/us/blog/your-wise-brain/201010/confronting-the-negativity-bias

Vaish, A., Grossmann, T., & Woodward, A. (2008). Not All Emotions Are Created Equal: The Negativity Bias in Social-Emotional Development. *Psychological Bulletin, 134*(3), 383–403. doi:10.1037/0033-2909.134.3.383

Chapter 6

Durlofsky, P. (2012, April 22). Maximizing Your Potential by Knowing Your Strengths and Managing Your Weaknesses. Retrieved from http://www.uploadinghope.com/2012/04/maximinizing-your-potential-by-knowing.html

Hodges, T. D., & Harter, J. K. (Spring 2005). The Quest for Strengths: A Review of the Theory and Research Underlying the Strengths Quest Program for Students. *Educational Horizons*, 190–201. Retrieved from https://files.eric.ed.gov/fulltext/EJ685058.pdf

Osmundson, L. (2018, March 14). Rejections, Tragedy, Caregiving— What Resilience Means to this Writer | Writing and Wellness. Retrieved from http://www.writingandwellness.com/2018/03/14/rejections-tragedy-caregiving-what-resilience-means-to-this-writer/

Rath, T., & Conchie, B. (2016). *Strengths Based Leadership: Great Leaders, Teams, and Why People Follow* (1st ed.). New York, NY: Gallup Press.

Rath, T., & Conchie, B. (2008, December 11). Finding Your Leadership Strengths. Retrieved from https://www.gallup.com/workplace/237038/finding-leadership-strengths.aspx

Rath, T., & Conchie, B. (2016, September 22). Global Study: ROI for Strengths-Based Development. Retrieved from https://www.gallup.com/workplace/236288/global-study-roi-strengths-based-development.aspx

So, T. (2008, June 18). Interview with Alex Linley: Strengthening the World (Part 1 of 2). Retrieved from https://positivepsychologynews.com/news/timothy-so/20080618803

Chapter 7

Allison, S. T. (2014, April 16). 5 Surprising Ways That Heroes Improve Our Lives. Retrieved from https://www.psychologytoday.com/us/blog/why-we-need-heroes/201404/5-surprising-ways-heroes-improve-our-lives

Allison, S. T., & Goethals, G. R. (2010). *Heroes: What They Do and Why We Need Them*. New York, NY: Oxford University Press.

Haidt, J. (2005, March 1). Wired to be Inspired. Retrieved from https://greatergood.berkeley.edu/article/item/wired_to_be_inspired

Poetry Foundation. (n.d.). *Andrea del Sarto by Robert Browning*. Retrieved from https://www.poetryfoundation.org/poems/43745/andrea-del-sarto

Chapter 8

Beebe, J. (Winter 2005). *Evolving the Eight-function Model: 8 Archetypes Guide How the Function-Attitudes Are Expressed in an Individual Psyche*. Retrieved from http://www.jungatlanta.com/articles/winter08-evolving-the-eight-function-model.pdf

Linda Berens Institute. (n.d.). Cognitive Dynamics. Retrieved from https://lindaberens.com/resources/methodology-articles/cognitive-dynamics/

The Myers & Briggs Foundation. (n.d.). MBTI Basics. Retrieved from https://www.myersbriggs.org/my-mbti-personality-type/mbti-basics/

Oklahoma State University. (n.d.). Figuring Out Your Type: Jung's 8 Cognitive Functions. Retrieved from https://osuwritingcenter.okstate.edu/blog/mbti-type

Chapter 9

Clance, P. R., & Imes, S. A. (1978). The Imposter Phenomenon in High Achieving Women: Dynamics and Therapeutic Intervention. *Psychotherapy: Theory, Research & Practice, 15*(3), 241–247. doi:10.1037/h0086006

Cutler, M. (2017, October 11). Featured Writer on Wellness: Megan Cutler | Writing and Wellness. Retrieved from http://www.writingandwellness.com/2017/10/11/featured-writer-on-wellness-megan-cutler/

Davis, J. (2017, September 28). Impostor's Syndrome and the Afflictions of the Accomplished. Retrieved from https://www.psychologytoday.com/blog/tracking-wonder/201709/impostors-syndrome-and-the-afflictions-the-accomplished

Francis, A. (2015, May 13). Emma Watson: I suffered from 'imposter syndrome' after Harry Potter - I felt like a fraud - CelebsNow. Retrieved from https://www.celebsnow.co.uk/celebrity-news/emma-watson-i-suffered-from-imposter-syndrome-after-harry-potter-i-felt-like-a-fraud-90219

Lambert, T. (2016, September 14). Featured Writer on Wellness: Troy Lambert | Writing and Wellness. Retrieved from http://www.writingandwellness.com/2016/09/14/featured-writer-on-wellness-troy-lambert/

Langford, J., & Clance, P. R. (1993). The Imposter Phenomenon: Recent Research Findings Regarding Dynamics, Personality and Family Patterns and Their Implications for Treatment. *Psychotherapy: Theory, Research, Practice, Training, 30*(3), 495–501. doi:10.1037/0033-3204.30.3.495

Neil Gaiman 2012 Commencement Speech "Make Good Art" [Video file]. (2012, June 9). Retrieved from https://www.youtube.com/watch?v=plWexCID-kA

Weir, K. (n.d.). Feel like a Fraud? Retrieved from http://www.apa.org/gradpsych/2013/11/fraud.aspx

Chapter 10

Buchanan, L. (2017, June 7). From Spiritual Journey to Coaching Practice to Successful Book | Writing and Wellness. Retrieved from http://www.writingandwellness.com/2017/06/07/from-spiritual-journey-to-coaching-practice-to-successful-book/

Helms, C. (2018, May 30). What Happened When This Writer Banned Herself from Journaling | Writing and Wellness. Retrieved from http://www.writingandwellness.com/2018/05/30/what-happened-when-this-writer-banned-herself-from-journaling/

Nielsen, J. (2011, September 12). How Long Do Users Stay on Web Pages? Retrieved from https://www.nngroup.com/articles/how-long-do-users-stay-on-web-pages/

Chapter 11

Bright, N. (2018, July 11). Featured Writer on Wellness: Natalie Bright | Writing and Wellness. Retrieved from http://www.writingandwellness.com/2018/07/11/featured-writer-on-wellness-natalie-bright/

Grant, A. (2018, March 1). People Don't Actually Know Themselves Very Well. Retrieved from https://www.theatlantic.com/health/archive/2018/03/you-dont-know-yourself-as-well-as-you-think-you-do/554612/

Oh, I., Wang, G., & Mount, M. K. (2011). Validity of Observer Ratings of the Five-Factor Model of Personality Traits: A Meta-Analysis. *Journal of Applied Psychology, 96*(4), 762–773. doi:10.1037/a0021832

Vazire, S. (2010). Who Knows What about a Person? The Self–Other Knowledge Asymmetry (SOKA) model. *Journal of Personality and Social Psychology, 98*(2), 281–300. doi:10.1037/a0017908

Chapter 12

Business Dictionary. (n.d.). When Was the Last Time You Said This? Retrieved from http://www.businessdictionary.com/definition/mission-statement.html

Chapter 13

Bernard, J. (2016, February 17). Featured Writer on Wellness: Jennifer Bernard | Writing and Wellness. Retrieved from http://www.writingandwellness.com/2016/02/17/featured-writer-on-wellness-jennifer-bernard/

Nightingale-Conant Corporation, & Dale Carnegie Training (Firm). (2004). Assertive Conflict Management and Negotiation. In *The 5 essential people skills: [how to assert yourself, listen to others, and resolve conflicts]* (p. 238). Retrieved from https://books.google.com/books?id=-zMVO-vyf UUC&pg=PA238&lpg=PA238&dq=the+5+essential+people+skills+Inact ion+breeds+doubt+and+fear.&source=bl&ots=j7S_v3k2rL&sig=6PWiP_ ftFFXbgrJAjjjWxc-aFcA&hl=en&sa=X&ved=2ahUKEwj38Kzh0tvdAhV iFjQIHYsjA3AQ6AEwCXoECAQQAQ#v=onepage&q=the%205%20 essential%20people%20skills%20Inaction%20breeds%20doubt%20 and%20fear.&f=false

Sienkiewicz, L. K. (2015, October 8). Featured Writer on Wellness: Linda K. Sienkiewicz | Writing and Wellness. Retrieved from http://www.writingandwellness.com/2015/10/08/featured-writer-on-wellness-linda-k-sienkiewicz/

Chapter 14

Berns, G. (2008, December 6). In Hard Times, Fear Can Impair Decision-Making. Retrieved from https://www.nytimes.com/2008/12/07/jobs/07pre.html

Chanel, O., & Chichilnisky, G. (2009). The Influence of Fear in Decisions: Experimental Evidence. *SSRN Electronic Journal*. doi:10.2139/ssrn.1522277

Foster, J. A., Rinaman, L., & Cryan, J. F. (2017). Stress & the Gut-Brain Axis: Regulation by the Microbiome. *Neurobiol Stress, 2017*(7), 124–136. doi:10.1016/j.ynstr.2017.03.001

Hadhazy, A. (2010, February 12). Think Twice: How the Gut's "Second Brain" Influences Mood and Well-Being. Retrieved from https://www.scientificamerican.com/article/gut-second-brain/

HeartMath Institute. (n.d.). Heart-Brain Communication. In Science of the Heart: Exploring the Role of the Heart in Human Performance. Retrieved from https://www.heartmath.org/research/science-of-the-heart/heart-brain-communication/

Heller, D. (2018, March 21). Some Gut Feelings Are a Red Flag, According to New FSU Research - Florida State University News. Retrieved from http://news.fsu.edu/news/2018/03/20/gut-feelings-red-flag-according-new-fsu-research/

Henwood, S., & Soosalu, G. (2014, October). The Three Brains of Leadership: Harnessing the Wisdom within. Paper presented at ILA 16th Global Leadership Summit, San Diego, CA. Retrieved from https://www.researchgate.net/publication/274699861_The_three_brains_of_Leadership_Harnasing_the_Wisdom_within

Hu, Y., Wang, D., Pang, K., Xu, G., & Guo, J. (2014). The Effect of Emotion and Time Pressure on risk Decision-Making. *Journal of Risk Research, 18*(5), 637–650. doi:10.1080/13669877.2014.910688

McCraty, R., Atkinson, M., & Bradley, R. T. (2004). Electrophysiological Evidence of Intuition: Part 1. The Surprising Role of the Heart. *The Journal of Alternative and Complementary Medicine, 10*(1), 133–143. doi:10.1089/107555304322849057

Chapter 15

Cesarini, D., Dawes, C. T., Johannesson, M., Lichtenstein, P., & Wallace, B. (2009). Genetic Variation in Preferences for Giving and Risk Taking *Quarterly Journal of Economics, 124*(2), 809-842. doi:10.1162/qjec.2009.124.2.809

Dohmen, T. J., Falk, A., Huffman, D. J., Wagner, G. G., Schupp, J., & Sunde, U. (December 2005). Individual Risk Attitudes: New Evidence From a Large, Representative, Experimentally Validated Survey. *Journal of the European Economic Association, 2005*(9). Retrieved from https://www.researchgate.net/publication/5023078_Individual_Risk_Attitudes_New_Evidence_From_a_Large_Representative_Experimentally_Validated_Survey

Kuhnen, C. M., & Chiao, J. Y. (2009). Genetic Determinants of Financial Risk Taking. *PLOS ONE, 4*(2), e4362. doi:10.1371/journal.pone.0004362

Kuhnen, C. M., & Knutson, B. (2005). The Neural Basis of Financial Risk Taking. *Neuron, 47*(5), 763–770. doi:10.1016/j.neuron.2005.08.008

Patel, M. S., Asch, D. A., Rosin, R., Small, D. S., Bellamy, S. L., Heuer, J., ... Volpp, K. G. (2016). Framing Financial Incentives to Increase Physical Activity Among Overweight and Obese Adults. *Annals of Internal Medicine, 164*(6), 385. doi:10.7326/m15-1635

ScienceDaily. (2018, September 21). No Risk, No Fun? People Who Take Risks More Satisfied With Their Lives. Retrieved from https://www.sciencedaily.com/releases/2005/09/050919081143.htm

Stoel, R. D., De Geus, E. J., & Boomsma, D. I. (2006). Genetic Analysis of Sensation Seeking with an Extended Twin Design. *Behavior Genetics, 36*(2), 229–237. doi:10.1007/s10519-005-9028-5

Thomson, C. J., Hanna, C. W., Carlson, S. R., & Rupert, J. L. (2012). The -521 C/T Variant in the Dopamine-4-Receptor Gene (DRD4) is Associated with Skiing and Snowboarding Behavior. *Scandinavian Journal of Medicine & Science in Sports, 23*(2), e108–e113. doi:10.1111/sms.12031

Vorobyev, V., Kwon, M. S., Moe, D., Parkkola, R., & Hämäläinen, H. (2015). Risk-Taking Behavior in a Computerized Driving Task: Brain Activation Correlates of Decision-Making, Outcome, and Peer Influence in Male Adolescents. *PLOS ONE, 10*(6), e0129516. doi:10.1371/journal.pone.0129516

Wolpert, S. (2007, January 5). How Does Your Brain Respond When You Think about Gambling or Taking Risks? UCLA Study Offers New Insights. Retrieved from http://newsroom.ucla.edu/releases/How-Does-Your-Brain-Respond-When-7680

Chapter 16

Hayton, J., & Cacciotti, G. (2018, April 3). How Fear Helps (and Hurts) Entrepreneurs. Retrieved from https://hbr.org/2018/04/how-fear-helps-and-hurts-entrepreneurs

Kerr, W. R., Nanda, R., & Rhodes-Kropf, M. (2014). Entrepreneurship as Experimentation. *Journal of Economic Perspectives, 28*(3), 25–48. Retrieved from https://pubs.aeaweb.org/doi/pdfplus/10.1257/jep.28.3.25

Chapter 17

No references.

Chapter 18

No references.

ACKNOWLEDGMENTS

My sincere gratitude to:

P. J. Dempsey, for her experienced input and assistance as editor. It's a blessing to have such a trusted eye to return to for my second nonfiction book.

Natalie Hanemann, for her careful copy edit, and for pointing out those things I would have missed otherwise.

Mary Story, for finding the typos no one else finds, and for always encouraging me no matter what I want to try next.

My cover designer at Damonza, who found such creative ways to keep the look consistent between my two nonfiction books and yet still gave this one its own personality.

My friend Donna Cook, who's request for me to speak to her editor's group led to the chapter on taking risks. I so enjoy having your support and being able to work with you on writing-related projects as we both travel this creative journey.

The writers who agreed to share their stories in this book—you are all inspiring and I thank you for your unique insights.

All those who read and support my motivational blog, *Writing and Wellness*—it's your future I hope to positively impact in some small way.

My family, especially Mary and Gerald, for giving of your time and energy to support all my writing-related events. It means the world to me.

Colleen M. Story is on a mission to inspire people from all walks of life to overcome modern-day challenges and find creative fulfillment. Her first nonfiction book *Overwhelmed Writer Rescue* is full of practical, personalized solutions to help writers and other creative artists escape the tyranny of the to-do list and nurture the genius within. Among other awards, it was named Solo Medalist in the New Apple

Book Awards (2018) and earned the Book by Book Pub Award for the best writing and publishing book in 2018.

With over twenty years as a professional in the creative industry, Colleen has authored thousands of articles for publications like *Healthline* and *Women's Health*; worked with high-profile clients like Gerber Baby Products and Kellogg's; and ghostwritten books on back pain, nutrition, and cancer recovery. Her literary novel *Loreena's Gift* was an Idaho Author Awards first place winner, New Apple Solo Medalist winner, and Foreword Reviews' INDIES Book of the Year Awards winner, among others.

Colleen frequently serves as a keynote speaker and workshop leader, where she helps attendees remove mental and emotional blocks and tap into their unique creative powers. For more information, see her websites at Writing and Wellness (writingandwellness. com), Writer CEO (writerceo.com), and her author website (colleenmstory.com), or follow her on Twitter (@ colleen_m_story).

33909674R00182

Made in the USA
San Bernardino, CA
28 April 2019